How to Be
a Comedy
Writer

Secrets from the Inside

MARC BLAKE

summersdale

D0470133

HOW TO BE A COMEDY WRITER

Summersdale Publishers Ltd
46 West Street
Chichester
West Sussex
PO19 1RP
UK

www.summersdale.com

Printed and bound in Great Britain

ISBN 1 84024 465 8

Contents

Introduction

ARE YOU THE funniest person in your office? Were you the classroom wag? Did you ever collect comics or *Mad* magazine? Is half your living room taken up with comedy DVDs, books and scripts? Do you watch comedy on telly and think 'I could do that'?

Comedy is big business nowadays. It seems everyone is either a comedian or polishing up a comedy script. There are whole TV channels devoted to comedy and in its scripted form – the sketch, play, sitcom or screenplay – there is greater demand than ever before.

So where to start? The good news is that all you need to begin on your comedy career path is the desire to do so. There are no comedy exams; no GCSE or City and Guilds qualification in the well-turned phrase, the witty jibe or the finely honed gag. Passion is your entry level requirement, plus a smattering of talent and the dedication to giving it a go. Providing you have these fundamental prerequisites, comedy, like all other forms of writing, is a craft you can learn.

After looking at how and why we laugh, this book explores the arena of live comedy, because more often than not the desire to be funny is accompanied by the urge to perform. To some, the idea of getting up on stage and reciting their own material may seem as sensible as a live autopsy, but do follow the section on stand-up: the focus is on the creation of the material rather than the performance. (Note: performers always refer to their jokes as material because, like a roll of cloth, it can be tailored to suit, it can be threadbare or it can be woven into a rich tapestry. Comedians like metaphors.)

From live comedy, including sections on characters, topical jokes and playwriting, I move to sketches, discussing the mechanics of sketch writing, as well as giving tips on how best to submit your material. Sometimes a sketch expands beyond its natural length and you find yourself writing a script. This is where the sitcom or the comedy drama comes in. Both these forms are examined in detail. Perhaps you wish to take your comedy to another level still – to the comedy screenplay (a blueprint for a film) – there's a section on that as well.

Then there's published comedy. Joke books, parodies and comedy guides are filling the expanding humour sections in bookshops. There's also the comedy novel, the longest form of comedy writing but a popular one: Terry Pratchett and Ben Elton are selling worldwide. I conclude with a section on marketing yourself as a comedy writer, dealing with writer's block and some advice on how to pursue an agent.

This book will not make you funny. Wait… come back. The question of whether comic talent is born or made is a difficult one. Some, like Peter Kay, Eddie Izzard or Billy Connolly were clearly never meant to be anything other than comedians, whereas other successful joke tellers like Bob Monkhouse or Jack Dee have had to hone their talent over the years. Ronnie Barker was as prolific a writer as he was a performer, whereas Ronnie Corbett's armchair monologues were scripted by David Renwick. Raymond Allen, writer of *Some Mothers Do 'Ave 'Em*, is a spontaneously funny man, whilst Simon Nye, the creator of *Men Behaving Badly*, has a more circumspect approach to life.

Whether you come to comedy writing with a natural skill or not, you will probably need a good couple of years to find your feet and to develop your writing style. My intention is for this book to inspire, encourage and act as a catalyst for your talents. Even if you complete all the exercises, I cannot guarantee you will end up funnier, but if the talent is there, you will stand a much better chance of making a living from comedy writing.

ays write from the heart.
- Strong central character
- Sub-plot?

THINGS TO CONSIDER
- Finding an agent
- Overcoming writer's block
- writer should always
- a notebook & pen.

Part 1
Comedy basics

Why laugh?

THE FIRST MENTION of comedy comes from ancient Greece. Aristotle tells us that in the towns of Megaris and Sicyon, the people were noted for their coarse humour and a sense of the ridiculous. After an evening banquet, the young men would roam the streets with torches, headed by a lyre player or flautist. This was called a *comus* and the band members a *comoedus*: the idea being to mimic the dramatic choruses which were popular at the time.

In later Greek mythology, comedy was recognised as being one of the nine Muses. They believed that a talent for wit belonged to the gods and could be spirited away at any moment – very impressive to be counted a Muse, as among the others there was epic poetry, music and tragedy.

So from these early beginnings we see that comedy has two functions:

1. to ridicule, parody or to prick pomposity – a way of letting off steam; and

2. something more creative – a constructed comic view of the world.

We can trace these two approaches throughout history from the court jester to Shakespeare, from farce to Vaudeville, and from variety to revue right up to the present day. Whether it's *Austin Powers*, the Pythons or *Little Britain*, there is a definite lineage of laughter. What all comedy has in common is that it mocks those higher in status; it exposes their foolishness and helps us to bond.

Humans are the only species who laugh. Forget the bared teeth of the chimp or the tittering hyena; we are the only ones to let rip with a snigger, guffaw or belly laugh. And we learn young. Babies learn to laugh from as early as eight weeks old and small children love to run about in shameless glee. Laughter is natural and healthy, good for releasing endorphins and boosts our immune system. It has practical purposes too. Humour has been used by the church and by medical practitioners – in the middle ages, priests in Bavaria used to get up and do a kind of *Carry On* routine to get the congregation laughing. More recently, in Bombay, a Dr Madan Kataria set up laughing clubs to create a sense of community where religious and economic differences could be ignored.

The two principal kinds of laughter are those that bind and those that separate us. Cohesion is vital in any culture and shared notions of what is funny pull us together. We laugh in superiority as we pull the rug from underneath a famous celebrity or politician. We laugh at the foibles of the opposite sex. We laugh at another's embarrassment. We experience hubris and *schadenfreude*. We laugh to deal with feelings of mortality – witness gallows humour or the sardonic wit of doctors and nurses. Laughter can be silly and nonsensical or cruel and heartless.

As some of these examples suggest, laughter can belittle others, such as with sexist, racist or politically incorrect humour. This mockery, born out of fear, creates a lesser other and puts them at arm's length. This is laughter as a defence mechanism, a way of protecting our perceived tribe. It is important, though, to discern between racist taunting and xenophobia, which is a dislike for foreigners. The latter is universal, as all countries seem to have that other nation who is the butt of the joke.

Here are some who like to laugh at their neighbours.
I'm sure you can think of more…

America – Canada
Britain – France
Spain – Portugal
Scotland – England
New Zealand – Australia
Germany – Austria
Greenland – Iceland

Forms of humour

JOKES WORK ON us in one of two ways. Either we *see* something incongruous or we *hear* something that strikes us as funny. Laughter is a physical response. Look at the terminology – I cried with laughter, I wet myself, I split my sides, I busted a gut. Watch an audience at a show; when the punchline arrives they jerk forward, smiles become roars and if the comedian is particularly deft they applaud or shed tears of joy.

We have similar responses to recorded forms, but what is unique about live comedy is that it is *immediate*. It has to strike hard and fast. It does not bear much repetition and it does not always travel well. We all, of course, perform live, with our friends. We tell stories, we mock one another and we develop running gags. The *craft* comes in taking that freshness apart and trying to recreate it. For that, we need to look at visual and verbal humour.

Visual humour

This category includes:

1. **Slapstick**
2. **Exaggeration**
3. **Repetition**
4. **Mimicry**

Slapstick

A slapstick was originally a kind of divided wooden stick, which was used to strike others, with the laughs coming from the humiliation and supposed pain inflicted (it's OK – no one in comedy ever *really* gets hurt). Mr Punch has one. This term has grown to encompass any kind of boisterous knockabout comedy, from Laurel and Hardy to the Marx Brothers to Vic Reeves and Bob Mortimer. It requires precise timing to elicit laughter.

Exaggeration

We respond favourably to exaggeration: something is larger than it ought to be – the huge kitten in the title sequence to *The Goodies*, for instance; or it is smaller – Lee Evan's shrunken suit. There can also be contrasts in age or height or class. It is the extreme that amuses. Mr Creosote from Monty Python's *The Meaning of Life* is indelibly marked on a generation.

Repetition

If an action is at first seen and then repeatedly brought back, this sets up a train of comic anticipation so that an audience knows what is coming, but not when. Verbally, this is known as a call-back; visually, it's a kind of signature. Think of Laurel and Hardy hitting one another. The laugh comes not the first time, but begins to grow on the second, so that by the time the sixth brick hits Ollie on the head, we are helpless with laughter.

Mimicry

Spitting Image used mimicry and the exaggeration of celebrities' or politicians' quirks to get laughs. Mimicry works well also for Rory Bremner, the cast of *Dead Ringers* and other impressionists. Spoof and parody often get tangled up in this one, but more on these later as they aren't solely visual forms.

There are also other cartoon-like devices in visual

humour, such as the inappropriate response (a deadpan look in the face of disaster), the double take (the comedian has to look twice to take in the information) and general gurning – but these are reactions, and are not really *written*. Consequently, they fall outside the scope of this book.

Visual humour is accessible to all, as there is no language barrier. It is memorable too; just think of what you remember from sitcoms and films.

Oddly, strip cartoons in newspapers rely almost entirely on verbal jokes. If you think of a strip there are usually three panels: the first one sets something up, the second confirms it and the third delivers the punchline. This is known as the rule of three and is one basic joke form I shall return to often.

Verbal humour

This category includes:

1. **Simple** – sarcasm, repetition, reversal and bathos

2. **Sophisticated** – satirc, parody, irony and farce

3. **Wordplay** – wit, puns, innuendo and comic analogy

4. **Others** – a) displacement, anachronism and anthropomorphism
b) the truth (a.k.a. gallows humour or black comedy)

Simple forms

Sarcasm has long been acknowledged as the lowest form of wit. Yeah, right. Whatever. Rather than an actual form of joke, sarcasm can be a mannerism or a pose. This is easy to adopt and is often practised on TV by any number of actors who have studied at the School of American Deadpan or by teens who know no better.

As mentioned, the repetition of words, or a call-back, can be effective. The first child in the sandpit to say 'poo' gets a laugh. Then he says it to his little pals outside the sandpit and gets more giggles, and by the end of the day it is the funniest thing in the world. Then he says it at home and gets a slap. Tough crowd.

When repetition grows up it becomes the catchphrase, which is employed by comics and in sitcoms to great effect – from 'I'm free' to 'I don't believe it' and, of course, 'D'oh!' By itself the word or phrase lacks meaning, but repetition gives it stature.

> **We all like being part of a group and a shared catchphrase gives us a sense of belonging.**

The call-back is also a tool used by stand-ups. This is a way of reincorporating information from an earlier comment, which becomes a marker for the audience, flattering them and including them in the story.

A comic reversal takes a given fact, concept or piece of behaviour and turns it on its head. Think of the classic 'going for an English' sketch in *Goodness Gracious Me* – where a group of young Indians behave badly in an English restaurant, instead of a curry house.

Bathos is a trivial anticlimax – a shaggy dog story in which an audience is told a tale expecting a twist but instead receives nothing. These would have once been told to you by your dad or perhaps a dull uncle who delighted in torturing small children. This style of humour has now almost died out, perhaps because the joke/no joke format results in a watery smile and a dull uncle punched senseless to the ground.

Sophisticated forms

Parody is an affectionate spoof of an existing form of entertainment such as a movie, play or book. It pays homage to its subject, gently sending it up while using it as a template for the humour.

Satire is more pointed, delivering a body blow to the status of an individual or an institution. Peter Cook's imitation of Harold Macmillan heralded the satire boom of the 1960s. *Yes Minister* is a brilliant satire on the workings of government and bureaucracy, whereas *Spitting Image* poked fun at any celebrity, minister or member of the royals. Satire has a polemic, an attitude that states that this is *wrong*, or that this person must be exposed to ridicule. By its nature, this employs wit and often irony.

Comic (and dramatic) irony means simply that the audience is aware of a hidden meaning. Watch any episode of *Frasier* and see him make decisions out of snobbery that are plainly going to have repercussions. We enjoy the irony because he fails to sense his predicament. The same was true of Basil Fawlty. We are above the pit, gazing down.

Farce works on a series of misunderstandings. It begins with a close approximation of reality but then develops into a series of improbable events and coincidences. Great farces include *Fawlty Towers* and the works of Ray Cooney, Joe Orton, Michael Frayn or Alan Ayckbourn. The important thing about farce is to make the reality consistent, so it seems not only possible but probable that a vicar will arrive at the very moment a lover divests himself of his pants.

Wordplay

Wordplay is a catch-all term to include any comedy that relies on the dual (or triple) meaning of words or phrases. This is one reason why the English language is apposite for humour. Take almost any word and it will have a number of functions; its meaning depending not only on the spelling but on the placement, pronunciation or inflection. The most subtle use of wordplay is wit, which is a rapid understanding of a situation resulting in an amusing retort. 'Quick-witted', 'living on our wits' – these phrases imply intelligence and when verbalised, as in the programme *Have I Got News For You?*, are highly effective. Wit can also be used in the written form, giving the author time to compose the most devastating put-downs.

The bad pun lives on among the elderly and captions editors for magazines, with the tabloids making

Puns are of a somewhat lower order. When we hear a pun, what do we do but groan? Not ideal conditions for humour.

daily attempts to reinvigorate the form. Sometimes they succeed, but more often than not your tabloid headline is tortuous or strained. This is a British peculiarity, but then in the UK humour is a default setting – even at this less than hilarious level.

The comedian Tim Vine is one of few who have succeeded with puns: this is because his buffoon persona and five-hundred-gags-an-hour approach proves that only aggregate can mitigate against their dreadfulness. More often the trouble with puns is that we see them coming. The emphasis placed on the offending word gives us time to anticipate it and therefore the surprise is lost. Rather than deal with the *sound* of words, it is better to create pictures with them; take us to other places, confound our expectations.

Innuendo is a playful part of wordplay. Based on implied smut, innuendo relies on the replacement of the sexual term with an inoffensive abbreviation, such as the word *it*. Does she like it? Does she want it? For the king of the *double entendre*, see the *VIZ* comic character Finbarr Saunders ('Fnarr fnarr!').

Innuendo is closely allied to camp, which trades in sexuality, homosexuality and transgenderism. Camp alludes to our sexual orientation – often teasing and mocking the nuclear family and its sexual mores. This has always been popular in Britain from BBC radio's *Round the Horne* to *The Rocky Horror Show*, *The Dame Edna Experience* and *So Graham Norton*.

Analogies or metaphors are often used as a comic comparison. One way to find the humour in a situation is to suggest that something is like something else, thereby setting up a conjunction of images in the listener's mind.

Other forms

Displacement is one of the most common devices used by comedy writers. The first piece of information allows us to presume a location, a set of people or a sequence of events. However, this has been carefully worded so as not to reveal what is coming – that we are in a different place, talking to a different person or have been otherwise misled. In sketch form this is known as the *pull-back-to-reveal*.

Anachronism takes us backwards or forwards in time and places objects or people in odd juxtapositions to their circumstances. *Blackadder*, *Red Dwarf* and *Futurama* use it well.

Anthropomorphism is the attribution of human characteristics to animals or inanimate objects and vice versa. An example of this can be found in the routines of Eddie Izzard when he inhabits the world of cats that spend time drilling behind sofas, or birds who are dismayed to find one of their own in a plane, in First Class, with a glass of white wine.

Finally, there is the **truth**. A short, blunt statement of fact can bring about the laughter response because of its mere audacity. 'You can't say that!' we think when the comedian says something outrageous – but you can, and he should: it's his job. This need not be a political statement; it can just as easily be an observation that we have made in our heads but not vocalised. The job of the comedy writer is to mine these nuggets and to present them to an audience ahead of the competition.

Telling the truth also encompasses the concept of black or gallows humour, which is concerned chiefly with mocking our mortality. We tell jokes about Princess Diana or Stephen Hawking not only because we are cruel and like adding insult to injury (although that's half the fun) but because we fear their fate may one day be ours. If you have ever been in the company of doctors or nurses you will know that their humour is scatological at best, grim at worst. In dealing with death and disfigurement every day there needs to be some kind of pressure valve, which may explain why they often muck about with bits of dead people (if any TV detective series is anything to go by). Gallows humour is a resignation to death. It's going to happen anyway, so we may as well make light of it.

Laughter:

- Boosts the immune system
- Helps social cohesion
- Dispels lies
- Deals with embarrassment
- Pricks pomposity; satirises
- Deals with feelings of mortality
- Can divide society with sexism, racism etc.

...ays write from the heart.
- Strong central character
- Sub-plot?

THINGS TO CONSIDER
• Finding an agent.
• Overcoming writer's block
• ...riter should always
• ...a notebook & pen.

Part 2
Live comedy

Stand-up

Origins

Stand-up comedy originated with the court jester, which dates the craft to medieval times. It was not a respected trade and they were treated roughly by their patrons. Their patched clothing was a result of abject poverty and the job was tough: if the king had had a bad day, the jester was often beheaded. Bet that wasn't in the job description. That said, the jester did succeed in creating a place in court for mirth and frivolity, an officially sanctioned way of offsetting the trials of life which persists to this day – except that our top comedians are now fêted and rewarded with vast wealth (no, we can't have Jim Davidson beheaded).

Modern stand-up comedy has its roots in the British music hall, which was the predominant form of public entertainment from the 1850s onwards. These purpose-built halls combined the pub sing-along, supper concerts and shows from the local municipal pleasure gardens. A chairman would introduce song and dance acts; eating, drinking and smoking continued throughout; and the audience heckled or joined in with their favourite songs. The halls spread like wildfire and professional performers would appear at several venues each night. Less a pub gig, this became more of a theatrical show and came to be known as 'variety'. It was almost killed off by radio and cinema.

In America, stand-up was big in the Borscht Belt – a number of upstate New York hotels which were home to a thousand crooners and Jewish comics. A couple of decades later these too were overshadowed by TV. The jazz/beatnik coffee-houses then bred a new kind of performer. Lenny Bruce was the progenitor of a new kind of confessional style of comedy that flowered in the 1960s and 70s.

Counter culture heroes like George Carlin, Robert Klein and Richard Pryor were scurrilous, provocative and breathtakingly honest about a country that was sending its young men away to be killed in Vietnam.

In the UK, the Establishment Club, founded by Peter Cook, boosted a satire boom, but traditional stand-up survived in holiday camps (thanks to Butlins Redcoats) and in the working men's clubs. Billy Connolly and Jasper Carrott came out of these, as did Bernard Manning and Roy

Chubby Brown. In the late 1970s punk brought a comedy revolution. Alternative comedy was nihilistic, misanthropic and offensive to the emergent culture of the Young Urban Professional. Instead of telling old style jokes, the new breed advocated feminism and non-racism and condemned the police. By the early nineties most comics had become much more apolitical.

Television coverage of stand-up has been on the increase since then and many more have flocked to the profession. Management agencies foster and exploit the talent and the idea of digging material out of your own experience is the default setting for stand-ups on the British, American and Australian circuits. The comedian is expected to be the renaissance man; part road warrior, part sage – an outsider who says the unsayable in an overfed and under-cultured world. Thousands of these outsiders can be seen at their annual trade fairs – the Montreal and Edinburgh Festivals.

There is also a strong surrealist strain in stand-up. From Tommy Cooper to Emo Phillips, the stage has always accommodated the madcap, the bizarre and the emotionally strange. In the early nineties, Reeves and Mortimer blazed a trail and subsequently Harry

Hill, Eddie Izzard, Dylan Moran, Bill Bailey and Ross Noble have won many admirers.

What makes a comic?

He strolls on stage, deliberate and confident, grabs the mike, faces the crowd and releases a volley of jokes. The audience instantly trusts him and waves of hilarity flood back and forth throughout the room. He raises his game, improvising, coming up with ever more wacky notions, leading us down comedy paths, teasing us, lulling us and seducing us before delivering his final comic bombshell. Then, while we're craving more, he's gone, slunk away into the night.

Or…

He shambles on, blinks, gulps, and delivers a lame opener. He does not acknowledge this – or he overcompensates. He continues with three or four more flat gags before rounding on an audience member for not laughing. His voice goes up, he quickens, his mouth full of cotton. Silence now. He ploughs on, miring himself deeper in his predicament. He's trotted out his big closing line and has nothing left but his wits. It's not enough. He starts to pick on the audience, poking around for any response. Someone wearily tells him to get off. He parries the blow but the floodgates have opened. Heckling unfolds into chanting and before you know it, a room full of sweating drunks are baying for blood. He is led off by the compere.

A good comedian seems like your best mate who's just wandered into the pub with some fantastic story to tell, but he's not. He's a stranger. Through sheer force of personality and beautifully written material he forges an alliance with his audience.

Transcribing material

Who is your favourite stand-up? Jack Dee? Bill Hicks? Jo Brand? Bill Bailey? Victoria Wood? Woody Allen? Tommy Cooper? All these have created successful followings on their personalities and on their 'take' on the world. To understand how stand-up comedy works, it's important to put it under the microscope.

In the pre-alternative days, there was a pool of gags which were purloined by all and sundry. Their originators were long forgotten and journeyman comics felt no compunction in lifting what they needed. This is no longer the case. Today's comedian or comedy writer would not only be ostracised for any such borrowing but would also see his career stalled as clubs picked up on the rumour. They create their own, out of their own personalities.

What did you learn? Does it look as funny on the page? Or does it seem flat now you haven't got their accent, facial expressions or physical movements to bring it to life? Does it seem improvised or constructed? Does the comic get straight to the point or are there numerous digressions? Does he or she use call-backs, repetition, exaggerations, analogies or anthropomorphism? Are they a truth teller or is it a flight of fancy? What gets lost in the translation?

> And this material obviously works. But how? Choose your favourite stand-up and transcribe some of the material from one of their acts. They're available on DVD and CD as well as video and cassette. Don't use double acts, speciality acts or character comics (more about them later) but write down every gag, digression and repetition. Do enough so that you can analyse it later – a page of A4 ought to be ample.

Put a slash after each punchline. Are these regular or does the comic go for a whole paragraph before the joke? Are there jokes within the jokes? Where the audience laughs make a note. Is it a gag or a piece of audience participation? Try to see exactly where the jokes come. Do you notice a rhythm?

It will probably lose a lot of the magic for you, but that's good because you are seeing the material through the comedian's eyes. Comics never find what they are saying funny (after all, they will have said it a thousand times) – their focus is on delivery, pace and timing; anything to nail the laugh.

The craft of stand-up is one of the most exacting in the comedy writing world. Everything must be, or must be leading to, a joke. Anything else is fluff. Twenty minutes is the length of a set and in this time the comic must keep continuously wrong-footing and surprising us. Any joke that does not earn its keep will be ruthlessly pruned and only the guaranteed belters will remain. Nothing is waste.

Writing stand-up for others

Many comedians write all their own material as a point of honour. This is because they have a unique take on the world and all its foibles, but what happens when they become famous and are asked to turn out a fresh hour of material each year for a UK/world tour? Or when the TV series takes off and what with all the other commitments – the after-dinner speaking, corporate work, voiceovers, radio and panel shows – when do they find the time? Have they still got the vision? I used to write for Frankie Howerd, who always used a team. I was amazed to find that amongst all the 'Oh no, missus' and 'No, yes, shut your face' asides he knew *exactly* where to place the jokes. I have since written for many household faces, some of whom credit writers and some who don't.

The best approach if you fancy writing for stars is to study their material and turn out a great page of jokes that might suit them. Then approach their agent or management with a polite enquiry by letter or e-mail. A web search will yield the management's contact details. Ten no's might lead to a yes. Through one chance meeting I ended up writing topical material for a famous name for four years.

Persona and status

The persona is how a comic presents himself to others and how he is perceived by them. We all choose how we present ourselves to the public. Usually this is a polite version of ourselves, but with comedians it is an act and sometimes one that is at odds with what they are like 'backstage'. The iconoclast can be as warm and endearing off stage as the buffoon or clown can be foul-mouthed (sorry kids).

Our public persona may be high status – judge, policeman or bank manager; or low status – road sweeper, charity worker or homeless person. Most of us fall somewhere between these extremes but a comedian needs to be clear about who he is. Peter Cook was a high status performer; Lee Evans is not.

In life, our status is variable. We are boss to some, worker (or drone) to others.

This lack of clarity does not work for the solo performer. He *must* be defined for the audience to know

Pick six of your friends and think about where you are status-wise. Are you the ringleader, the social secretary, the jester, the moral barometer or the runt of the litter? Maybe you're something else entirely?

who he is. The comics in the diagram below are equally funny, but in different ways. These are clear *types* who give out a simple message to the crowd as to why they are funny. If an audience does not know who you are then they will be distracted. If they are distracted they are not listening and if they are not listening then they will not laugh.

Status table

HIGH STATUS (We laugh with them)	Cynic
	Polemicist
	Gagsmith
MIDDLE STATUS	Genial nice guy/girl
	Camp
LOW STATUS (We laugh at them)	Surrealist
	Loser
	Buffoon/clown

High status

The *cynic* is a misanthrope who rails at everything. No one escapes his scathing views and his disapproval at a world that has let him down.

The *polemicist* is equally miffed, but his anger has a focus and a target. He has something to say and by God you are going to hear it. His comedy makes points and offers alternatives. He is often highly politicised or principled.

These are as rare as *gagsmiths* are common. This brand of joke teller is often a motormouth alpha male who will end up as a chat show or panel game host. These guys and girls can quell any rough crowd and have a million put-downs at their disposal (e.g. 'Don't heckle me – I don't come to where you work and kick your broom.'). They are all high status, standing above us, as we laugh with them at the follies of the world we inhabit.

Middle status

In the middle is the genial nice guy or girl; a warm, smart individual who neither berates us nor takes us to another comedy planet. Those who succeed in this category are in the minority and often go on to become comedy actors. Also in this section are camp comedians. Although they seem brash, provocative and outrageous (and very high status) this bitchy type of humour is actually quite brittle. There is a vulnerability to it.

Low status

On the other side of the comedy coin are the losers, clowns and surrealists. These are the ones who look funny the moment they hit the stage. The loser is the odd kid at school, the freakish individual who was bullied throughout his teenage years and who failed to indulge in sexual congress. These bizarre types take their peculiar traits and make the most of them, turning failure into hilarity and tragedy into pathos. The buffoon or clown will do anything for the laugh, from slapstick to gurning to pratfalls. The silly and ludicrous are his stock in trade, but don't assume this only means juvenilia; there are modern acts that use clowning or buffoonery in a much cooler way.

Surreal comedians create a world in which we are tourists. It is our world, but viewed from an oblique angle. *Non sequiturs*, off-the-cuff improvisations and odd juxtapositions abound, often challenging the norm of what is or isn't funny. This means their material is more individual and harder to 'get'. In the early days of their career, lower status comedians find it harder going, but when they do succeed, they do it big.

Can you be more than one of these types? Yes, but you must keep to your status band. If you stray too far into the other realm you will confuse the audience. I have oversimplified the audience reaction to comics into two types: laughing with and laughing at. However, that is the essential difference between the high and the low status comedian.

I do not include character comedians or impressionists in this list, as they play many roles and so can fall into any of the bands. Some, such as Lenny Henry, Victoria Wood or Billy Connolly, are even harder to compartmentalise. This is because their extensive TV and film work as comic actors has changed our perception of them. Lenny Henry has moved from clown to polemicist. Billy Connolly started out as The Big Yin – a foul-mouthed, folk-song-singing fool – but went surreal and then political. Victoria Wood, the archetypal genial nice girl (though her work has always had bite) plays a plethora of roles.

> **Write the names of twenty famous comedians. Define and divide them into the bands. It ought to be fairly clear who is where. These bands represent comedic attitudes. Clear and focused. Once the comedian has identified this, he has a hook to hang his material on and can now develop his material to suit. Yes, the persona is somewhat limited, but once the comic reaches wider success, he will broaden out to become a more fully-rounded character.**

Targets and attitude

All comedy has a target, be it the government, C-list celebrities or our own behaviour. Identifying the point or the victim of your comedy is the quickest route towards getting the joke right. At the same time, concepts like intolerance, avarice or 'the culture of spin' are too nebulous to pinpoint with ease. It's easier to name names. If you're writing topical material, the public figures are obvious, but what about when you are dealing with people who have stupid ringtones? Who are they? Rich people? Chavs? Kids? Or is this the latest sad addition to the repertoire of the office joker? Whenever you come up with an idea for a joke, you must first define your target.

Maybe your humour is self-deprecating? Good, then let the target be you. Be consistent. If you jump between the things you hate and the things about yourself that you hate, the audience will lose focus. Comedy is a blunt instrument and when you skewer pomposity you only get one shot. Make it count. When you are searching for material, first isolate and underline the target in each and every remark. Try going back to the famous comedian's material that you transcribed and underlining the targets. They are clear.

Attitude is vital to any comic or piece of comic writing. Just read the think pieces in your Sunday newspaper. These are really no more than a slight comic riff on something that has angered the journalist (and which he or she has managed to sell to a national newspaper). Anger is a mainspring for comedy and it's true that dissatisfaction with the status quo is one thing that many comedians share. It is not, however, the only emotion that drives us. Iconoclasts are rare, and other feelings like worry, frustration or sheer confusion are equally valid as triggers. They have less of the heat of pure rage but remember – anger burns out quickly. It's often suggested that comedians lose their edge as they get older and benefit from their success. The public feels cheated that their hero is still attacking dog mess and the Labour administration when we know they are living in a million pound home in Primrose Hill.

You will find your attitude changes with each topic. Some things enrage, others leave you cold. The skill of the comic writer is to be able to manufacture attitude at will. If you don't care, how much do you not care? If 4x4 SUV drivers don't annoy you, then how about cyclists? Or getting at other drivers from the point of view of the 4x4 owner? Everything can be switched around to suit the purpose of the writer.

Remember:

- All comedy has a target.

- Define your target.

- Underline your target to ensure that it is clear.

- Use your emotions. Anger helps you to select targets but also use worry, fear, confusion, frustration.

How to write stand-up material

If you are thinking of doing stand-up yourself then your material is all around you. Review your day and make a list of the things that annoy you. Be as personal or as general as you like. Who or what is pushing your buttons right now? List twenty topics on a sheet of A4. Now strike out half – you can always return to them later. Order the remaining ones into a top ten. Are there a few more that aren't earning their keep? Get rid of them as well. Keep the top five.

Who or what are the targets? Put each topic heading on a separate piece of paper. Now come up with ten facts about each topic; we will be making jokes out of this information. Are there any facts or expressions that lend themselves to a dual or second meaning? Can you make an analogy? An exaggeration? Can you turn the ideas on their heads? Question every fact and put your thoughts down next to them. Don't worry about writing jokes straight away. All that's needed are ideas.

Now ask 'What if…?' Let your imagination soar. You have fifty bits of information to work with here. Here are some examples.

What if… smoking was banned but everyone became addicted to sweet cigarettes?

What if… you really did have eyes in the back of your head?

What if… London transport was run by Germans?

Don't worry how ridiculous these may seem. You'll know which ones are fruitful either because you'll laugh immediately or you'll keep returning to them.

Once you have lots of ideas you can begin to order them into the set-up, which is the first informational sentence, and the punchline, which is the joke. Together these are often referred to as a 'one-liner'.

The first part is your nugget of stated fact. You will see this in the transcribed material you wrote. They always open with a clear statement, e.g.:

Set-up:
I was taught to drive by a former hairdresser.

This tells us only what we need to know. A hairdresser taught me to drive – how is that going to be different to a normal instructor? The second sentence is the wordplay, exaggeration or visual dislocation.

Punchline:
Every time I looked in the mirror, he held another little mirror behind my head.

Can you think of another punchline?

How about writing a joke about parents who push their kids about in those mini off-road buggies? Do the kids talk about the kind of mileage and road-holding they get? Take the audience into the conversation between two infants.

Can you make a joke from the following set-ups?

> 🖊 My local supermarket has banned obese people.

> 🖊 My girlfriend's a waitress.

> 🖊 I bought an ex-police dog.

There is not a lot of difference between this and the old 'Doctor, Doctor' or 'My mother-in-law's so fat…' kind of joke. The observational style of humour is the same, but the sensibility is different.

Perhaps you prefer a more surreal approach in which hatred or disgust does not play a part. Here it will be in the juxtaposition of ideas that the comedy arrives. Ask yourself what might happen if, instead of a mobile phone, you carried a musical birthday card? If you dated a mute, how would you know if she was giving you the silent treatment? Why is there always one empty tank at an aquarium? Why is the Bible made out of Rizla papers? What about helium air bags for cars? How do dyslexics cope with texting – or a Ouija board? The possibilities are limitless. Seek out the unusual.

Once you have written a few jokes – ten will do – check through them. Have you found the funniest image? Keep working at the joke until the best punchline arrives. Perhaps you'll get the joke first and work back to writing the set-up (in the tightest, most economical way). It's like a Haiku or, if you want the Western version, think of it as like playing a fruit machine. Cherry, cherry, lemon. You must keep pulling the handle to get the right line-up for the payout.

Keep adding ideas into the mix until the right one comes along. Keep rewording the joke – not just the punchline but the set-up as well. You might try writing down your ideas, cutting them out, throwing them in the air and seeing what juxtapositions come out of it.

Topical material

You may have sourced your material from the newspapers. That's fine. There is a market for topical jokes. This has its pluses and its minuses. On the plus side, the topical comedian relates immediately to an impressed crowd. He could only have thought of it on the day. On the minus, nothing dates so quickly. Topicals go stale after two or three uses unless you can apply them to another situation.

There is a constant demand for up to the minute jokes – for after-dinner speeches, by comics and TV presenters, and for radio and TV sketch shows. The snappy one-liner and biting satirical comment will always find a home if it's placed in the right hands. Topical material is a source that constantly needs replenishing.

Are you up to date on party politics or local government issues? Do you have strong views on Europe, the USA or the Middle East? Do you trawl celebrity gossip in the tabloids? Don't worry if you have no particular allegiances – topical comedy is about commenting on the news, finding an attitude and hitting those targets. This does not require a huge amount of knowledge about current affairs.

Go out and buy a tabloid newspaper. Skim through it. The stories are always told in bite-sized chunks, often with an overt moral agenda. A supermodel or pop star is admonished for his or her excesses, a politician is caught in a knot of deceit, a football star is having three-in-a-bed sex ('He Scores in the Bedroom!'). It's much the same story every time. This means that it's possible to create a database of jokes that you can reuse.

The format for topical material is the same as that of writing one-liners: in fact it's easier, since you have more clear and simple information to hand. First list the top ten stories that you wish to tackle. Pick out the targets.

Skim and scan several dailies in order to get the facts. Broadsheets are less helpful for this in that they go into detail. You need the quick hit, the outrageous allegation, the biased opinion.

Work out the prevailing opinion. Are we praising or condemning this person? Do you want to go against the grain and support someone who you feel is being maligned? Topical comedy is about saying the unpalatable – the things the papers *don't* say. You can, however, get it wrong. You might write a joke that offends current opinion.

What is 'politically correct?' Over the last twenty years our culture has spawned a set of behavioural precepts that are backed by corporate and state law, stating that no one can be offended. Words and/or behaviour that might upset gays, women, non-whites and the mentally or physically challenged have increasingly become heretical in today's Western society.

This is either a sensible drive towards equality or a curtailing of free expression that invokes the Inquisition, the suppression of Galileo and the tyranny of Communism. Whatever your view, it is an issue that cannot be ignored. Comedy subscribes to no dogma, but what might once have been merely in poor taste can now have legal consequences. You may privately think that women are worse drivers than men, or use words like spaz, mong or lard-arse (the correct terms are Scopey, mentally challenged and salad dodger) but this thinking can have repercussions. The option of self-censorship is the only tenet of comedy. Say what you like and don't be afraid to exercise free expression, but remember that with this comes responsibility.

Topicals, however, usually do not get above taking the mickey out of sportsmen, politicians or the legion of bottom-feeding quasi-celebrities who daily pollute our TV screens. Because you are using existing material you are pretty much free from libel and slander – but if you do depart from the news and start to make up fresh accusations then it's a different situation.

Developing the facility for writing topical gags takes a little time, but you will find it easier than creating other kinds of material. For one you don't have to do all that hard work on the persona – you can simply lift an off-the-peg attitude. You can also connect with other news stories and events. Is it a special time of year – Hallowe'en, Christmas or Easter? Are there a number of awards ceremonies on right now? Sporting events? All these can help to connect and to firm up the gags. Look for the clichés and use them. 'Spending more time with his family.' 'Wrong kind of leaves.' 'Celebrity unable to appear due to exhaustion.' Use analogies, exaggerations, reversals and dislocations, satire and sarcasm.

If you find yourself writing dialogue, go to the section on sketches.

Remember:

- Topical material makes fresh comments on the news.

- Use the tabloids to pick out targets.

- You only need use what's in the story.

- Connect stories and use cultural phenomena.

- Isolate the target every time.

- The only censor is yourself.

- Deliver quality and volume.

Road-testing your material

Comedians use their audiences to try out new stuff because you cannot fool the crowd. If it's funny they laugh; if not, you get silence. A comic will test out his new material three or four times, but if it doesn't work he will place it elsewhere in the set, rethink it, put it away for a while or dump it.

As a new writer you don't have that luxury. If you have found someone who's great at buoying you up and who is willing to give an unbiased opinion on your comedy, then keep them close. If not, you may get a false opinion. A spouse might humour you to save your feelings and we all feel bad about saying 'I don't get it'. Plus, if you read jokes right off the page you are coming to it cold, which is distancing. One way novice writers try to get round this is to slip into the material down the pub once people are a bit oiled. In this way you'll get more of a genuine reaction.

You might try recruiting a comedy partner – someone you met at a comedy club or evening class. This partnership allows both of you to test out your individual material, and shouldn't be confused with a double act. If and when you do find such a person, take care. Establish the parameters of when he or she wants to hear the material and what kind of feedback you do or don't want. Comedy is a fragile thing, as are comedy egos, and a poorly-timed critique can set you back. But remember, it is hard to get honest criticism for comedy and if you do, welcome it with open arms.

Feedback

✐ Be clear about the amount of involvement you want.

✐ Pick a mutually good time and place for trying out material.

✐ If you have asked for criticism be prepared to accept it.

Building a set

The scattergun approach to writing jokes is great if your material is so excellent that each gag is a polished gem. Otherwise, comics tend to clump their jokes together into routines. This means a string of jokes on one topic, after which they move on to the next. Typically, these routines are a few minutes each and when bolted together form a set. A set is twenty minutes of material and is the standard performance required of a professional comedian, although this can last up to half an hour or even forty minutes.

For this twenty minutes the weak jokes will have been discarded (comedy triage) and the best cherry-picked. The process of building a set takes about a year, but stage time is built up by doing many shorter five- and ten-minute slots. Writing jokes does get easier, plus for the working comic there are the incidentals – the facial expressions, acting, impressions and improvisations – which all add to the pot. Sometimes comedians are criticised for doing the same material, but to cast it aside would be like a decorator spending a year as an apprentice and then chucking away his brushes and paints. The truth of it is that audiences hardly ever remember the material – they remember the comic.

Within a set, it's vital to have a strong opening and closer. This bookends the performance, allowing for more considered ideas to find their space. This does not mean inserting weak gags as, like athletes, comedians must always play at the top of their game. However, not every joke can be a pant-wetter and there has to be time for the audience to catch their breath. Comedy needs a rhythm and this means natural peaks and troughs. Think of it as being like sex if you must: there has to be foreplay, rhythm, intimacy and a big finish. And you should be leaving your audience wanting more.

A note on explicitly sexual material. If you open with it, where are you going to go? What do we do after sex? Sleep? Smoke a cigarette? Run off to the pub? Whichever way, it's all over. It's a peak. If you have twenty minutes on sex then let the audience have it, but otherwise it is best to build *toward* intimacy. Scatological material can also offend, which is fine, but in the bigger comedy clubs people usually eat during the show. If you put them off their food, takings will go down and the promoter might start looking for a scapegoat.

Try to organise your ideas so that they lead towards a conclusion. Use call-backs – looping the idea round itself or repeating a phrase from earlier on. Keep the surprises coming but harbour your biggest belter for the end. Never think of encores. If you have jokes put aside for this, they ought to be in the set. Promoters and audiences always recognise excellent material.

Remember:

- Random gags are fine but all must be of outstanding quality.

- You must have a strong opener and closer.

- Build towards intimacy.

- Scatological jokes should be done after people have finished eating.

- Allow for peaks and troughs.

- The encore should be in the set.

The open mike

All comedy writers ought to attend an open mike night. These are evenings devoted to new talent, performed in five- or ten-minute chunks by performers new to the business. They are held in draughty, badly-lit rooms above pubs, usually with free admission (so the audience has no investment in the show), sometimes without a stage and sometimes without a mike. If you are lucky there is a half-decent compere who will absorb any flak and who will focus on making it easy for the novices. They will be told not to overrun but inevitably will and the evening will drag on to the bitter end, with the only remaining audience being friends of the comics, tourists or those bizarre types who are married to pubs. But it's not all fun.

The quality of performers will vary from those who ought to be sectioned to those who have a degree of confidence and some promise. On the whole, the experience will be not be earth-shattering. The open mike night is the entry level for all comics and it's a good way to put your comedy writing to the test. You should never blame an audience for a poor reaction unless they are not specifically there to be entertained (I have heard of gigs where the 'promoter' simply unplugged the TV and announced the gig – thus somewhat irking the hundred Spurs fans about to watch the match).

There is a waiting list for open mike spots, often running into weeks or months. In larger venues you will be given the opportunity to perform for free only once or twice a year. Your local listings magazine will have details of these nights; if you're not sure if they are open mike nights then look for shows with more than five names on the bill. Expect to be booked in several months away and don't expect anyone to ever return your calls.

If you want to perform, first hone your material to a tight five minutes (about twelve gags). Bullet point it, or use one key word to remember each joke. Time yourself. Most comedians wear a watch with a stopwatch or vibrating timer. Decide on what to wear that will make you feel comfortable on stage.

On the night, show up early, find the promoter and let him know you are there. Ask the compere where you are on the bill and tell him how to pronounce your name. When you are on, don't overrun. Use your watch to keep to time – the audience might love your every utterance, but the promoter and the other acts will be willing you off.

Afterwards, thank the promoter for the slot and enquire about another. Now you're hooked. The first hundred gigs are the hardest.

Remember:

- Be punctual.

- Learn your material off by heart.

- Don't expect calls or e-mails to be returned.

- Be polite to venue owners

- Let them know you are there.

- Don't overrun.

- Bring a diary in case they have return dates.

Editing

Say you've written a stand-up routine and you've tried it out a few times. Perhaps you've thought ahead and recorded the gig on a dictaphone so you have an accurate record of the audience response. There were laughs. You refined it, tried it out again, got more, carried on building – but you are not bringing the house down. This is partly down to your nascent performance skills but also because of the material. As this book focuses on writing, here are some of the things which can go wrong on that score:

Too obvious. The jokes are not far enough away from the set-up to create that moment of surprise. The thinking is not unexpected and the audience are getting there ahead of you. Keep rewriting and thinking of more apposite punchlines. Are you relying on wordplay or puns and not being visual enough?

Too obscure. The punchline or set-up is not connecting. Either the information is too specified or too personal. You must make your world accessible. Have you introduced elements or inconsistencies that no one will believe?

Too long. Is your material too wordy? Is it taking forever to get to the punchline? Have you introduced irrelevancies? Strike out all extraneous words which are not the joke or leading to the joke. Be brief at all times.

Not true. Is it not a fair or true observation on life? Is it not fresh enough? There are many subjects covered by hundreds of comics out there and there are bound to be common denominators. Some topics are hackneyed, such as smoking, tube travel or the insistence that Welsh people are prone to ovine intimacy. Comedy relies on breaking down stereotypes, not reinforcing them.

General poor reaction. Perhaps you don't have a strong enough supply of jokes. The laughs are there but there are no peaks. An audience needs to trust the comedian's writing and to know that there is something fresh, true and hilarious coming. You must ruthlessly prune out all the duff gags.

Character comedy

ANOTHER TYPE OF live comedy that is becoming increasingly popular is character comedy. More a branch of the acting tree, the character comedian inhabits a role and gives a lecture as that person to the audience. When combined with other performers this becomes sketch comedy (more on that later).

There isn't that much character comedy in the clubs at present – partly as it's so much harder to buy into. There's no context, plus wigs, costumes and props look out of place in places where the punchline is king. A character needs familiarity and repetition before audiences can warm to him. But that's not to say that character cannot excel – The Pub Landlord and Otis Lee Crenshaw were both Perrier Award winners – but it is tougher. For this reason many character acts choose to perform at the Edinburgh Fringe or in sketch shows, which are predisposed to the weird and wonderful. These are fertile breeding grounds for the fledgling TV career. Matt Lucas of *Little Britain* and Steve Coogan of *Alan Partridge* fame both began in the clubs.

Although writing character comedy is slightly different to straight stand-up, I wish to address it here, as it is performed live. Instead of an attitude or a target, you start from a personality trait, an overheard phrase or some observed behaviour. You might begin with a relative or friend, someone you've seen on holiday or someone from your daily life.

Look around you and describe two odd traits of the people you work with – unsettling, isn't it? Northern comics from Les Dawson to Alan Bennett to Victoria Wood to Peter Kay have fixed the foibles of the folk around them, whereas down south, Harry Enfield, Paul Whitehouse and Lucas and Walliams have all found eccentric oddities.

> There are no hard and fast rules about what will work and what won't. A character might remain stillborn despite your creating a whole world for him, or a silly notion that becomes loved by all.

Sometimes these characters remain one-dimensional – a punchline or catchphrase: 'You ain't seen me, right?', 'Nice', 'I'm a lady' – and sometimes they become fully rounded creations like Ali G.

Characters are a blend of stereotype and archetype. They need to be recognisable enough for a broad audience to relate to them, but different enough from us all to be fresh and exciting. They are, though, exaggerations. This can be shown in speech, dress or mannerism. Often characters have a degree of social ineptness about them. Comic characters in film have a view of themselves that contrasts sharply with their true nature. Austin Powers believes himself to be a great lover. Ali G – a white man from Staines – is convinced that he is black. David Brent sees himself as everyone's friend when he is their boss and a lousy one at that.

These incompatibilities are their fatal flaw.

Start writing your character by asking yourself about their obsession. Probity? Fidelity? Getting laid? Think simply. One word will do. Then create circumstances for them to fail. Put obstacles in their way. Don't give them what they want. Characters are more storytellers than gagsmiths. They have a passion to tell us about the terrible things that have happened to them. It is in the gap between their view of reality and the obvious truth that comes laughter.

Character works on a high degree of irony. We know that they are not 'real' but we buy into the vision created by the writer. The character often has a highly inflated opinion of himself or herself, which is continually undermined by the truth. Characters in comedy are a shared joke with the audience, one in which we gleefully anticipate their downfall.

Catchphrases are hard to manufacture but the closer you stick to the truth of the character – writing from inside his head, the more likely you are to find one. Phrases like 'I'm the only gay in the village' or 'Suits you, sir' sum up a character with a few well-chosen words.

Write a one-page monologue for your character, addressing the audience in a lecture format. This is an ideal reason for their being on stage. They have come to impart some vital information. Again, it ought to come across as someone bursting into the pub to tell us the latest disaster, only this time it's the village idiot telling it.

If you can write six different short monologues for your character then you are probably onto something.

Remember:

- Create an archetype not a stereotype.
- Write from inside the character.
- Look for hobbies and obsessions.
- What is their fatal flaw?
- Catchphrases come from repeated behaviour.
- Write a one-page monologue to test out the character.

Live sketch shows

A LOT OF live sketch comedy in the UK is geared towards the Edinburgh Festival in the belief that television producers will see it and turn it into a TV series. This does happen but for every *League of Gentlemen* there are ten struggling sketch companies. I will cover sketch writing in more detail in the recorded comedy section, but for now here are a few pointers for the sketch show.

- There ought to be no more than two or three speaking parts in a sketch – ideally, the dialogue exists only between the comic and the feed.

- Sketches are based on a comic premise, a series of complications and a resolve which ties up the loose ends (more on this in Part 3).

- Often characters misunderstand one another or end up talking at cross purposes.

- Remember to include a varied cast of people and acting styles so that if an audience tires of one sketch or performer, then at least they know someone or something different is coming up soon.

- One hour is a good time slot to aim for. Any more and even the greatest comedy pales beside the urge for a bar break.

- Sketches are quick to write but not to write well. Even the Pythons and Spike Milligan had a high failure rate. All you can do to try to improve your strike rate is to ruthlessly edit the sketches that fail to get laughs. The difficulty is sometimes not with the individual sketches, but what happens to them on aggregate. This is more of an issue of theme, known in the business as format. You might want to try basing your sketch show around a theme, so as to give a sense of continuity.

- Recurring characters or situations help to anchor the show.

There are many venues and pub/fringe theatres which can be hired by the night to put on sketch shows. Alternatively, try the room above your local pub or rent the studio space at your local arts centre. Sketch nights are a great showcase for performers and writers and it is through this that your comedy writing career may flower.

The comedy play

MAYBE STAND-UP DOESN'T do it for you, or you have found that sketch writing has its limitations? But lurking in there is the big idea. If this is the case you might want to try your hand at writing a play. Alan Ayckbourn, Ray Cooney, Alan Bennett, Terry Johnson and Michael Frayn have all ridden high with successful plays in London's West End – not to mention Noël Coward, Oscar Wilde, Joe Orton and George Bernard Shaw.

The advantages of the successful play are manifold: it's repeatable, so you can revive it; it's sustainable, so it can have a long run instead of a one-off; and it's adaptable, so it can be rewritten for radio, TV or film.

Plays are not only put on in the West End but also in theatres all across the country and across the globe. A hit like *Educating Rita* or *Art* will be playing somewhere every day of the year. The playwright also has a bonus in that his words are sacrosanct. There is very little rewriting. The director and actors must work with what you have put on the page. Their job is one of interpretation – but with that comes the responsibility of getting it right.

Luckily, as with a live sketch show or with stand-up, you can tinker with it in the early stages by putting it on in a fringe theatre or arts space. Plays are relatively immediate. Once written and cast, a production can be mounted in weeks. You can run it for a few nights or a few weeks – it's up to you (although if you want reviews, the latter is advisable as many publications will only review a play with a decent 'run').

The modern comedy play is a comedy of social mores and manners. Hits such as *Art* or *Closer* (a wealthy friend buys a ridiculous piece of art; the interwoven love lives of a London quartet) use dark humour to show a more complex comic view of the world. A situation is important. You are not merely writing about characters who just chat. The story must lead somewhere, propel us forwards into further and deeper complications.

A small cast is important: enough plot can be generated from a trio without recourse to farce. The play gives you time to explore themes, whether they are political, social or behavioural. You can offer argument and discussion. There must, of course, be a resolution as comedy, even when it is brutal, does tend towards the happy ending.

Play running times have shortened since Shakespeare's day, with *Art* coming in at a slim

90 minutes. Despite attempts in the 1970s to take 'theatre to the masses', it remains a middle-class amusement (this is reflected in ticket prices) and your choice of subject matter will reflect the interests of your public. You may choose between a one-, two- or three-act play, but it has been said that the length of a play depends on the bladders of the audience. An hour and a half is about the longest a crowd can go without relief, so do plan a suitable interval.

The skills you will require for playwriting are those of characterisation, plotting, dialogue and wit. As with much comedy writing, you will only discover if

> **A play is not just a convenient hook for all those jokes that didn't work in stand-up; it should consist of real, living, breathing characters in a dramatic predicament. They don't find it funny: we do.**

you have an aptitude for it by doing it. A warning: do not blame the actors if your production stinks. As the adage goes, a good play will not be ruined by bad acting, but a bad play cannot succeed with even the best.

Plays are constructed in acts and scenes, which ought not be too numerous. Scenes take place over a short time, usually one part of the day or night, and are constricted to fit what is needed for the characters to move the plot forwards. An act is several scenes put together to create a dramatic whole with a definite beginning, middle and end. Further acts may occur days, weeks or even years later.

There is no need to tell the actors how to read their lines, as tone and inflection ought to be implicit from the words on the page.

You can use **(Pause)** for pauses or *italics* for emphasis. **Ellipses**, too, carry a certain weight… and sometimes a **dash** is useful –

– if dialogue is overlapping. The length of a speech varies from one word to a whole page. CAPITALS can only be interpreted as SHOUTING.

Buy plays from French's bookshop or online to get an idea of how they look in cold hard type.

> **When writing the play, at the beginning of each scene put a brief description of the place, time of day and what props are necessary. The rest is dialogue, assisted ably by *stage directions*, which instruct the actors and director as to what is happening. Keep these simple.**

Putting it on

The National Theatre regularly puts on comedies from new and established playwrights, but economics dictate that the musical is currently the predominant form in the West End. *The Producers* is brilliant musically, theatrically and comedically and was, of course, originally a film (1969). *My Fair Lady* or *Pygmalion* has had more makeovers than Madonna. At the time of writing we are living in an age of nostalgia, with all its retreads, re-imaginings and the strip mining of the recent cultural past. This will pass, but it is indicative of the conservative nature of producers.

The theatres themselves are old, uncomfortable (and sometimes dangerous) and subject to high ground rent. All this makes putting on a comedy a big risk. The importing of US or soap stars will guarantee a frisson of excitement (i.e. bookings) but it's hard to find a comedy that anyone can love when the competition is multi-channel TV or a comfortable cinema at a quarter of the price.

You can, however, tour a play in the provinces and still earn from it. There are numerous arts centres and small independent theatres across the country, most of which are locally funded and have superb facilities. A well-written comedy can run in studio spaces and at festivals all over the world (e.g. the plays of John Godber). If you have written a play, take it to your local fringe venue. Most have an artistic director to whom you can go with new work. Alternatively, hire out the space and put it on yourself. This DIY option is becoming more popular. Consider the following:

✎ You will need to hire the technical crew. Good sound and light operators are a godsend. The venue will have their own, but do not expect them to be included in the rental agreement. Most are happy to tech your show for a small cash sum per night and the usual rule is to keep them sweet. A badly teched show can be a disaster.

✎ The hire of the space is either for one slot (which may only be two to three hours including the get-in-and-out) or for an agreed number of days or weeks. You may get a reduction on a longer run, but do you really need it? Be clear on how much rehearsal time they offer, when they allow a tech rehearsal and whether they penalise if you overrun.

Check that box office staff and front of house are included. Also, do they sell tickets online and, if so, what percentage is given over to the marketing company? It's unlikely you will profit but how much do you want to give away to a third party?

Check their client list, i.e. supporters of the theatre who will receive programmes, e-mails and mail-outs. Apart from your family and friends, you are relying on their audience base. This affects:

The percentage. Either you agree on a straight rental deal – which means you pay them an agreed fee and you take whatever comes in the door – or you have a split. This second option means you pay less upfront, but anywhere from 20–40 per cent of the take goes back to the theatre.

Printing and publicity. The cost of photographs, flyers and mail-outs are often borne by the artist. You can make this as cheap or as expensive as you like. With increased technology, we can all print off a decent A4 page, but A3 or A1 posters cost money.

Props and costumes, even if 'model's own' or sourced from local charity shops (which they inevitably are) are also your responsibility.

Why not video it as well? That way you'll be able to see in the light of day how successful a performance has been, and to see the failings as well. It's from these we learn.

ways write from the heart.
- Strong central character
- Sub-plot?

THINGS TO CONSIDER
• Finding an agent
• Overcoming writer's block
  writer should always
  a notebook & pen.

Part 3
Recorded comedy

Screen basics

RECORDED COMEDY DIFFERS from live performance in that you do not see the fruits of your labours immediately. Whether it's a sketch, sitcom, comedy drama or screenplay, you are not there in the room with the viewer to witness the effectiveness of your work (except at studio recordings, but you only have limited 'tweaking' time). You have to make an educated guess. You have to hope that it's funny with the only clear result being when a broadcaster recommissions your show.

This is why there are script editors. These are seasoned professionals – usually writers themselves – who have been through this process and who have developed a good ear for what is going to work and what won't. Trust them; they want to get it right as much as you do, because if a show flops then there is egg on everyone's faces.

Sketch shows are known as 'broken' comedy because they are fragmented – lots of quickies and vox pops (short pieces to camera) and sketches bolted together with a strong format or theme. This is opposed to the sitcom or comedy drama, which has a continuous storyline and the same characters each week.

The screenplay is a much bigger investment of time and effort and I will cover that at the end of this section.

Broken comedy

Sketch or quickie?

Sketches are pieces of dialogue rather than the monologue of stand-up comedy. Two comedians, or the straight man and the feed, tackle a problem, explore its complications, and end up with a resolution. This ought not last more than three to four minutes, or the same numbers in pages of script.

A quickie is a sketch that lasts for less than a minute and is often a visual or an aural one-liner. The most common term for this is the *pull-back-to-reveal*, mentioned in Part 1, which means that the camera starts on a close-up or on a two shot (there are two people in the frame) and then, as the term suggests, pulls back to reveal the joke. This is often a change in size or location. Think of John Cleese reading the news in the sea in *Monty Python*. It works well on radio as well. Imagine two people discussing politics in the hallowed halls of Parliament but as the conversation develops we realise that they are actually in a zoo (OK, maybe that's not much of a stretch).

The quickie can also be a simple catchphrase like *The Fast Show*'s 'This week I have mostly been eating yoghurt'; or a statement, as in *A Bit of Fry and Laurie*'s oblique vox pops. Quickies can also be the visual equivalent of the rule of three, where someone does something, then it is repeated and then finally twisted to create the joke. If you have ever seen the fish-slapping dance in *Monty Python* then you will have seen a good (and surreal) example of the visual quickie.

The sketch has three parts – the premise, the complication and the punchline. The premise is the idea, the concept which peaks our interest and has us thinking of what will happen next. The complications are the escalations that flow from this (maybe through parody or analogy) and the punchline or resolution is the twist to flip it over at the end.

Learn from the best

A man walks into a shop and asks for four candles, but is misheard as asking for fork handles. The shopkeeper eventually twigs, but every following item is equally confused by these *double entendres*.

(*The Two Ronnies*)

A man asks if this is the room for an argument but he is rebuffed. He then realises that if the man is contradicting him then he must be in the right place.

(*Monty Python*)

A one-legged man applies for the role of Tarzan.

(*Not Only But Also*)

A great premise will hook the viewer in. The complications follow the logic to absurd ends. A notable *Alas Smith and Jones* sketch had several shipwrecked sailors discussing who ought to be eaten first, with each one explaining why it shouldn't be them. With an idea like this the sketch almost writes itself.

Sketches should never outstay their welcome. Five pages is ample time in which to get across your idea. Always read out and time your sketches. There are myriad ways of approaching sketch writing but if you are not already churning out ideas by the bucketload I suggest you start by using the exercises mentioned earlier on in generating material. Think of what annoys you at the moment. List ten things and map out the aspects around them. How could you turn this into a scenario?

What if…

…tramps were franchised out to needy posh towns?

…there was a charity to save ageing rock musicians?

…men used more than three tenths of their brains?

Types of sketch

There are two ways of writing sketches. The first is where the punchline comes fully formed. You know the ending and all you have to do is to work backwards to the point where you introduce the characters and the idea. Sadly, this happens all too rarely and most of us are stuck with the second method which is to work forwards. This is when a comic conceit occurs and we start to develop the complications. The parody, analogy, metaphor or exaggeration falls into place until we try to round it off. We hunt for the twist but when it eventually comes, it still has a kind of ersatz feel to it.

The reason for this is that life doesn't have punchlines. In trying to create a comic ending, we are going against the grain. Some shows give up and don't bother; *Monty Python's Flying Circus*, *Smack the Pony* and *Big Train* all de-emphasised or removed the punch (so you are in good company) but others never fail to round off the sketches (*The Two Ronnies* or *A Bit of Fry and Laurie*). Most sketch shows aim for a balance of the two.

If a sketch fails to resolve itself, leave it alone for a couple of days and then return to it with a closer eye on the characters rather than the joke itself.

Rule of three and lists

The rule of three is a common device in comedy (think of those newspaper strips). The first thing that we see or hear sets up the idea, the second confirms it and the third confounds us. Why does it work? It's in the way we receive information. The first and second items are enough for us to form a conclusion, to accept something as the norm. The third defies the expectation. The rule of three also has a wonderful rhythm to it. I was this, and this... and then *this*.

Surprisingly its ubiquity has not made this device stale and you will still hear thousands of variations. Note down a few from some comedy DVDs. There are comedians and comedy routines that have exploited this concept so well that they have developed five or even more extensions to one central idea.

List-making is another way of running with one basic idea. Once you have the joke, list several alternative variations and keep going until you run out of steam.

What if old people were as badly behaved as the young?

They might...

... have wheelchairs up on blocks outside their houses.

... wear Burberry flat caps and anorak hoodies.

... do graffiti in watercolour.

... go 'happy slapping' and record it with a Brownie box camera.

... get tanked up on cocoa and hang about charity shops.

... go ram raiding in their motorised chairs.

Parody and satire

Parody, because it copies an existing form, is the most common type of sketch attempted by the newcomer. Paying homage to another art form (movies) was what kicked off Woody Allen's and Mel Brooks' careers. Other proponents are the Comic Strip team, the Zucker brothers (*Airplane*) and Mike Myers with *Austin Powers*. You already have the characters and story, all you need do is exaggerate the truth about the genre.

Satire is more thoughtful and has a political or social point to make. Peter Cook made his name writing satirical sketches and later continued to pester society with his brainchild, *Private Eye* magazine. Later came *Spitting Image*, *Yes Minister*, *The Day Today*, *Brass Eye* and *Bremner, Bird and Fortune*. To write a satirical sketch your targets must be well defined and the accusations you make well thought through. It's not enough to call the government a bunch of w*****s. You must know exactly why they are w*****s and explain it clearly to us. It's a fine line as to what's libellous – you'll find out when the writ arrives.

Analogy

The concept of being hooked on something is a common starting point for a sketch.

'I started young, just a few, then I got hooked. It was all day every day, and then I was stealing to fund my habit. I got caught or I tried to kick the habit, I went through hell and then detox and now I'm clean.'

This cycle is so familiar that it can be used as a metaphor for more innocuous things. The comic analogy or metaphor is clever; you have to *get it*, to be in on the joke. This means that in writing about it you must be clear at the outset what parallels you are drawing. You cannot mix the metaphor. The imagery must remain consistent. For example, you might be writing about a posh homeless person trying to obtain a cardboard box in the country 'for weekends'. That's fine, but he will not necessarily be a drunk or drug addict as well. He may well wish to entertain his gentlemen friends of the road but the analogy is about posh people in reduced circumstances – not about drink. Be clear and logical at all times.

Cross purposes

Sometimes two people in a sketch can be talking at cross purposes, with both unaware of the other's discomfort. We must, however, relate to one of them. Usually it's the one who speaks first (often the straight man). The conversation progresses with ever more ludicrous exaggerations that muddy the waters. Sometimes there is an abrupt turnaround in which the talker accepts the oddness of the other – in effect joining in the madness. Sometimes they leave as perplexed as when they began, but always the humour comes from them defending the truth *as they see it*. This has been a successful sketch device from *The Frost Report* through *Morecambe and Wise* and *The Two Ronnies* to *French and Saunders*.

Relocation and reverse

Write a sketch about anything – a man ordering a meal, a woman drying her hair, a couple feeding their cat – but set it somewhere else or reverse the sex roles. Placing events out of their natural settings always breeds ideas and you may strike a rich vein of humour. The idea mentioned previously, of old people being anti-social, is a reverse.

How about these...

The man orders fish, but both he and the waiter are underwater.

A man talks about drying his hair in the way a woman would do.

The couple are zoo keepers and are soppy about their tiger.

Anachronism and anthropomorphism

Set a sketch in the past, but with up to date language and gadgets. Imagine what it would be like today if we did not have medicine, the phone or the washing machine.

What do mayflies talk about in their one day on this planet? Do wasps have anything to say to each other apart from 'nice jumper'? When chimps are typing, what do they come up with before the works of Shakespeare? If you are writing about animals it need not be played by two blokes in costume. Animation has come down in price, and animals, birds or insects can be animated on a reasonable budget.

Radio or TV?

If you are thinking of radio then the best place to start is to listen to it. A lot. BBC Radio 2 and 4 have a large output of comedy shows and these will give you a good indication of what's current in this genre. You will find that radio is the natural home for the sketch. With only voice, music and sound effects the listener can be transported to any place or time and into all manner of weird and wonderful worlds. BBC radio has a number of shows for which the novice can submit his or her material. These shows are politically flavoured and usually topical. You will be expected to offer material up for free on a regular basis before any real interest is shown. It's a great feeling to hear your name read out in the list at the end of the show.

The market for TV sketches waxes and wanes. Once there was *Monty Python*, *The Goodies* and *The Two Ronnies*, then *Spitting Image* and *Alas Smith and Jones*. *Harry Enfield and Chums* and *Absolutely Fabulous* came next, then *The Fast Show*, *Smack the Pony*, *Big Train* and *The League of Gentlemen*. More recently *Little Britain* and *Monkey Dust* arrived on our screens. They are a perennial format. Sketch comedy is sold successfully around the world and garners awards such as the Golden Rose at Montreux.

The drawback to broken comedy series is that they burn out quickly. Rarely do sketch shows survive more than three seasons: not merely because the talent wants to move on, but because it's hard to sustain the level of comic brilliance. This does, however, mean there is a big turnaround, so you have plenty of chances to get in there with your ideas.

Themes and formats

The theme of *Goodness Gracious Me* was Asians in Britain. *Little Britain* is a pot-pourri of off British characters played by two actors. *Does He Take Sugar?* (BBC Radio 4) was about disability. The theme encompasses the show.

The format is the collection of elements that go to make it up. From the outside most formats look the same – a bunch of quickies interspersed with running characters and longer sketches. However, it's your approach that counts. A simple analogy: you have eggs, flour, milk, lemon and sugar: the theme is a pancake, the ingredients are the format. If you want to develop your own half-hour sketch show then you need to be in the pancake business.

The theme of my BBC radio series *Whining for England* was an A–Z of moaning about our nation. The format was that I divided the letters into six parts, and had a monologue and sketch for each one (some letters were harder than others). There was a song each week. It seems simple, but it took me four years of being turned down to get to it.

Sketch shows are also often centred on the particular talents of a comedian of the day (e.g. Lenny Henry, Kenny Everett or Catherine Tate). Sometimes the show pretends not to have a format (e.g. *The Goon Show*) but if you listen to it regularly, you will find that there are running characters or certain styles of sketches. Nothing is totally free form.

There have been sketch shows set in mock news networks, pirate or satellite stations. The media often comes up because of its easy access to stories, but this is a fairly hackneyed setting. It is not possible to sell a portfolio of sketches alone unless your writing is so unique that they simply have to create a format around you.

Some tips on sketch writing

1. Do not write expensive scenes with cavalry or elephants if writing for TV. Budgets are always low and everything is done on the cheap.

2. Write for two speaking parts, three at the most.

3. If you are writing for a specific show, keep to their brief.

4. You can use the real names of the comedians you are writing for.

5. Number each page and put your contact details on a header or footer.

6. Try to write visually, even if it's for radio.

7. Props always go wrong. Costumes are expensive.

8. Send out your best work – don't keep it in a drawer for yourself.

Spend some time on this. List all the sketch shows you've seen and heard on radio and TV and study their themes. You will see common ones emerging (e.g. spoof documentary). How does your idea differ to what already exists? Why is yours special? Before an entertainment head commissions your show, he or she will have to decommission something else. Make yours sing. Think of a viewer switching channels. Why would he pause when he came to yours?

Sitcom

SITCOM IS ABOUT characters who do not change or grow. They are trapped with people they hate, in jobs they despise, in circumstances which annoy them. This means that they are in constant conflict, without which there would be no comedy.

It is also always a half-hour show. There are sometimes longer specials, but these rarely work as effectively and tend to be the Christmas editions. Half an hour is a comfortable time slot in which to introduce a plot, develop complications and resolve the story, leaving your characters back where they started.

The cast is a small one, usually a set of friends, relatives or workmates. Think of *The Royle Family*, *Steptoe and Son* or *Friends* – everyone knows everyone else intimately; their foibles, their likes and dislikes, and more importantly how to press their buttons.

Types of sitcom

The most common forms of sitcom are set in the workplace and in the domestic arena. *Are You Being Served?*, *Drop the Dead Donkey* and *The Office* were all set on the shop floor. The workplace has clear demarcations; boss and employee, colleagues or rivals. The domestic sitcom has a long and illustrious history from *Steptoe and Son* to *Bread*, *Men Behaving Badly* and *The Royle Family*. Broadly speaking, all sitcoms fall into either one of these camps.

Variants include the 'gang show' sitcom (e.g. *Dad's Army*), 'one man against the world' (e.g. *One Foot in the Grave*), 'fish out of water' (*The Fresh Prince of Bel Air*) and 'chalk and cheese' (e.g. *The Odd Couple*). All these are explored in more detail in my book *How to be a Sitcom Writer*.

Creating characters

Sitcom characters are not just a bunch of crazies who fire zingers at one another. They are believable people trapped in lives of desperation. Often there is one who rises above the pack to become the memorable focus for the show and this I call the monster character. At the heart of many sitcoms there is a tyrant or whingeing fool, a cruel boss or incompetent husband, a gullible moron or a pontificating bore. These are people who either do not recognise boundaries or who trample them in their search for power.

Try thinking about some people, celebrities, for instance, who you actively dislike. What traits do they share? List ten of them. Chances are they will be similar to those of the sitcom monster. Now focus on people in your life who have got your goat. What was their relationship to you? Ex-boss, workmate, school bully, ex-partner? Sibling or parent? What traits do they have that push your buttons?

We have a love/hate relationship with sitcom monsters because they are *contained*. We know that they are a creation and this acts as a safety measure which allows us to distance ourselves from them. If the embarrassments they suffer or create were to happen in real life, it would most likely be unbearable.

We get characters from our lives. You cannot crib from TV. If you have not anchored the character in any kind of real, living presence, then you run the risk of writing a stereotype. Readers are heartily sick of 'feisty' women, 'duckers and divers' and other generic types – so why give them the ammo to destroy your project before you've started?

Writing a sitcom is a big project and character must be at its core. Yours might be an amalgamation of people you have known, or exaggerations of some of them; the closer the better. Think about your family. Who else do we know so intimately? Pick someone and write some notes about how they deal with trouble and the pressure points which drive you insane about them. Do they have a sense of humour? A fatal flaw? A saving grace? What does he or she want out of life? Could they become a sitcom monster character if they were put in the right circumstances?

It's a good idea with characters to create a CV for them. It doesn't have to be 100 per cent based on their inspiration: it only has to feel real. Pick someone you know and write down the following:

- When and where were they born?

- Who were their siblings? What was the relationship between them?

- What events helped to form their character?

- Where were they schooled and to what degree?

- To whom did they lose their virginity?

🖋 What were their first and subsequent jobs?

🖋 Who is their current partner? If none, list failed conquests.

🖋 What did they attempt and fail at?

🖋 Where have they been on holiday or in their gap year?

🖋 What car do they drive? What kind of pets do they have?

Relationships

Sitcoms are also about the conflict between small groups of people. Before you decide on this emotional arena, it's worth taking a few minutes to jot down all the relationships we have in life. Most of these involve family, friends, neighbours or professional relationships.

You will probably find that the family relationships take up the lion's share, and this is reflected in the fact that domestic sitcoms are the most popular. Even if we live in broken or extended families, we all have, or have had, experience of parents, siblings and grandparents. If you have put boyfriend and girlfriend on your list, note that this is a prototype man and wife relationship. What about the master/ slave relationship that you have with your boss, a teacher, even your doctor? Whatever characters you write, it is best to conceive of them as a family. The boss is a tyrannical father (Mainwaring in *Dad's Army*). There is often a passive or harried moderating mother figure in sitcoms (Neil in *The Young Ones*) and the other characters often fall neatly into warring sibling roles (Tim and Gareth in *The Office*). Base your sitcom on the family model and all its intrigue, petty disputes and in-fighting and you can't go far wrong.

The trap

In real life, once we fly the nest, we make our own choices, ideally learning from our mistakes and growing to become well-rounded people. Not so in sitcom. The veneer is there, but the characters remain immature, selfish and self-important – essentially children. *Friends* is a wonderful example of this: these are adults with adult problems, but instead of facing them they retain their adolescent angst and kowtow to peer group pressure that says 'We are the centre of our lives'.

Try listing all the things which can trap a person; things which put us in stasis and lock us into our behaviour patterns. Think of Del Boy, whose poverty keeps him struggling, or Frasier, who is bound by duty to his father. These characters may have any number of traps in their lives, but one might be predominant.

Plotting

Plotting is problems. Sitcom plots rarely concern an alien invasion or a messy divorce, but are more likely to be about school grades or an impending driving test. You must face the character with his or her fears. The best way to identify this is to refer back to what your character wanted out of life. If it was safety, then introduce risk. If it was power, then threaten this. If it was comfort then remove it; if it was love, then deny him it. Our characters are in limbo and any problem that cuts to the core of them ought to be one that destabilises this.

This initial problem is called the *inciting incident*. A simple piece of information arrives, upon which he or she must act. The comedy then arises firstly in his *reaction* to the event and then in his subsequent *actions*. His behaviour will then be consistent to his character. What sitcom characters often do is to make an obviously bad decision. This is comic irony. We the audience cover our mouths in gleeful anticipation of where this is going to lead. Sitcom at its best has plenty of these 'Oh no' moments. We cringe at Brent, Rigsby, Meldrew and Monsoon because to them their actions are rational; to us they are ludicrous and embarrassing.

Where do we get plots from? Try making a list of real-life incidents that might affect your characters in any one day. It's endless, isn't it? If you are struggling, you might be inspired by news events, but don't stick too closely to the facts. Use only the inciting incident – the headline – and see where your characters can take this story.

Watch other sitcoms and note the plot's inciting incident. If your characters are strong enough you ought to be able to use any of these plot ideas and make them your own. The story should deepen in complexity as a result of bad decisions, before finally resolving itself. This resolve must

> **Use things that have happened to you or your family – but be aware that to stick religiously to the facts can make your characters act against their natural inclination.**

come from within the story and be true to the nature of the character. No *deus ex machina* allowed.

Writing a sitcom

A sitcom can be one of the most rigorous and rewarding kinds of comedy writing and most of your energy ought to be expended in getting the above right. A sitcom can be set anywhere – on an oil rig, in a judge's chambers or on the moon – but it is not this that will keep the viewers glued. It must be the characters and how they interact with one another. They are slightly larger than life and ideally there is one monstrous character who lacks the embarrassment gene.

Once you lock all this down, the process of writing a script is a fairly quick one. Ten days to a month is about all you need to spend on a first draft. This is called the pilot episode, because it introduces all the characters to a new audience. It is a good idea to then put this aside and write another.

The reason for this is that the first script will have been too clunky to sell; full of exposition and too much about the situation rather than the characters inhabiting it. The second script, based on a second plot, must feel like a well-organised party. You are introduced to everyone without being confused by numbers. They are interesting people. You laugh, enjoying them for the moment and leaving early before it all turns pear-shaped. This might be a slightly tortuous analogy, but remember, the script editor has never set eyes on your work before. It must grab his attention.

Check that each character is coming alive. Get into each scene or piece of story as late as you can (this is why there are so many entrances and exits in sitcoms) and get out early. Don't write jokes. Let your characters live and breathe and let the comedy flow from this.

> **Before you send out a sitcom script – which should come in at around 6–7,000 words – read it out loud. You could also get some friends or even actors to do so.**

There is more about selling your sitcom in Part 5, and much more on this in my book, *How to be a Sitcom Writer*.

Remember:

- Plotting is problems.

- Plot is about facing the character with his or her fears.

- Plots require an inciting incident.

- Get into and out of each scene as soon as possible.

- Use newspapers and real-life stories but don't be dogmatic.

- Don't write jokes; write real dialogue.

- Sitcoms can be set anywhere but must be limited by character.

- Read your script aloud.

Comedy drama

COMEDY DRAMA IS a difficult genre to categorise. Critics claim that it's comedy that isn't funny and drama that's not very dramatic. Comedy drama does encompass these dangers, but it's also a real TV ratings grabber. The main difference to sitcom (apart from the running time) is that comedy drama always has a narrative. This means that there is a story or number of plots and subplots running across the episodes. These will often climax in a cliff-hanger to keep us tuning in the following week. The main story is plotted so as to form a resolution at the end of the series, usually with just enough loose ends to keep us hanging around for the next time.

Unlike sitcom, comedy drama is a television hour, which comes in at around 50–55 minutes with commercial breaks and/or trailers. There are also a number of core characters whose lives are held together with a common job, purpose or family scenario. The following are examples of comedy drama in Britain and the US:

BRITAIN	US
Cold Feet	The Sopranos
At Home with the Braithwaites	Six Feet Under
Life Begins	Desperate Housewives
Shameless	Ally McBeal

Whereas sitcom's major function is to produce laughs, comedy drama aims to give a more rounded picture of life. As well as humour, there is raw emotion, dramatic denouement and resolution. The dramatic view of the world says that people will triumph in the worst of circumstances and that there is justice and a natural sense of morality. The comedic view says that in the best of circumstances we will still screw up. Comedy drama does want to have its cake and eat it – but when it succeeds, it does so in a big way.

In creating a comedy drama, a lot of thought must be given to the format. It seems so simple – series like *Footballers' Wives* do exactly what they say on the tin – but this is deceptive. A huge amount of thought has gone into finding a fresh scenario, location and just the right combination of characters to make the whole thing work. Above all you are looking for promise and sustainability. The fresh idea must not only grab the attention of any producer, but show real scope.

Write the first episode and map out the rest of the series in short paragraphs. Create character biographies (a CV for each of them) and indicate how the show will progress into series two and three. You'll know you are onto a winner if when you show the idea to people, they think it's so brilliant and obvious that it should have been done before.

Comedy drama is generally the preserve of the drama writer, and to progress well in this area, it's a good idea to study drama writing.

Creating a series proposal

To sell the idea to a broadcaster, you will have to give them more than one script or a one-off episode, no matter how brilliant it is. This is because commissioners are not looking for single comedies (they would be better suited to a film) or two parters (the preserve of drama), but a series.

This means a sustainable set of characters (or protagonists – a term used for characters in drama) in an intricate and interesting situation that is likely to throw up varied comic scenes week in week out, and ideally over years. This is where the series proposal comes in. This is a document which describes your whole show in a few pages. You must provide the following:

- a full description of your protagonist(s)

- a series of brief character breakdowns of your main cast

- a guide to the setting and the situation of your comedy drama

- a full synopsis of the first episode

- a brief synopsis of the other episodes in the first series

- an indication of how series two (and even three) will progress the idea

Problems with comedy drama proposals

The following are some problems that crop up in writing series proposals:

Cliché. The characters are generic thirty-somethings, stereotypical northerners or duckers and divers. We have all seen them before.

Confused. The narrative flow is not clear from your proposal. We cannot follow a clear arc. What is happening to these people?

Overcrowded. The writer is uncertain that his characters are interesting enough and so has piled in many plots or extra people to cover this up.

Too close. There has been a recent example of something similar that has been successful (or has failed) in the genre.

Limited scope. Doctors, lawyers and the police are staple diets of TV drama. This is because their lives crash into many others on a regular basis. You may have thought laterally, focusing on graphic designers or care workers, but there isn't enough to retain our interest.

This location and its characters are too specific and a broad audience will be unable to relate to them.

Unfunny. The series idea does not throw up enough comic potential and might be better written as straight drama.

Screenplays

THE SCREEN COMEDY has been a staple diet of cinema ever since Charlie Chaplin ate a hat and Buster Keaton was surrounded by a falling building. As the talkies arrived and narrative structures developed, comedy changed with it. Slapstick was replaced with more ingenious farce and social comedies, but certain rules still remain.

Comedy must be a life or death struggle for the comic actor, but not for the viewer. In the blackest or sickest of comedies no one dies for real. It's a comedy death. You can hit someone round the face with a pan forever, but we know it doesn't really hurt. This is why children shriek at clowns – and why we laugh at Peter Sellers, Ben Stiller or John Prescott.

Comedy also pokes fun at institutions, attacking and denouncing false values. It is idealist. If the world were perfect then there would be no comedy. To this aim it always tries to be contemporary. As mores change, so does comedy, which means that it dates more quickly than other art forms. The broader the comedy the more chance it has of lasting, but let's not forget that comedy does not travel well.

It finds it hard to get past geographical, cultural and language barriers. The US studios are well aware of foreign markets and this is why their products are aimed at the widest possible audience. Their comedies always aim at universality.

Genre

The history of screen comedy is studded with classics, even if they are rarely rewarded with Oscars. Some of the genres in comedy include:

Caper comedy

The heist, the last job gone wrong and the elaborate swindle has been around since talkies began. They require panic, peril and speed in order to throw the characters into a spiral of defeat and eventual redemption. Examples of the genre are *Toy Story*, *Some Like it Hot*, *The Blues Brothers*, *Raising Arizona* and *Lock, Stock and Two Smoking Barrels*.

Romantic comedy

These stories are inevitably about an apparently mismatched couple who take the whole movie to figure out that they were made for each other. The rule is they always end up together, the plot being a map of all the possible ways of keeping them apart, via internal or external sources. Worth catching are *His Girl Friday, Four Weddings and a Funeral, When Harry Met Sally, There's Something About Mary* or *Notting Hill*. They more or less always end with a wedding.

Spoof

Spoof or parody picks on another genre and sends it up, the more serious the better; which is why the actors must play it straight and must not wink at the audience. Classics include the monumental dumbness of *This is Spinal Tap*, the silliness of the *Monty Python* films, the hilarious parodies of Mel Brooks and the Zucker brothers. In more recent times, *Scary Movie, Austin Powers* and *Team America* have been added to the list.

Satire

Satire applies ridicule and irony to our behaviour, as well as our institutions. *The Graduate, M★A★S★H* and *Sullivan's Travels* were as effective in mocking post-war society as *Magnolia* or *Happiness* is at doing the same to our hedonistic contemporary world.

Black or gross-out comedy

Comedy has always pushed the boundaries of taste and decency. Sex, murder and death are all fair game, from *Kind Hearts and Coronets* to *The War of the Roses*, *Heathers*, *Fargo*, *Gremlins* and *American Pie*. Again, no one really gets hurt. It just feels like it.

Dumb

Knockabout comedy has no more intent than proving that stupid is as stupid does. The puerile and infantile are deified in such movies as *Duck Soup* or *Mr Hulot's Holiday*. Laurel and Hardy's work is a masterclass in dumb and other great examples are: *The Nutty Professor*, *Animal House*, the *Pink Panther* series, *The Jerk*, *Porky's*, *Wayne's World* and *Dumb and Dumber*.

Characters in screen comedy

The one aspect comedy protagonists share is they are driven by a blind desire. The dramatic character can step back and be aware of his situation but the comic one can't. He lives in the here and now and has no real idea of its flaws. Even if he docs have some inkling, as in the many films of Woody Allen, he is still unable to identify a solution. Inspector Clouseau was obsessed with being the world's best detective. The comedy arises from the reality that he wasn't.

When the obsession is a person, this becomes romantic comedy, as in *There's Something About Mary* or the *Bridget Jones* movies. The converse can also be true, in that the romantic leads might not actually be after each other. Examples include *When Harry Met Sally* (the possibility of male/female platonic friendship) or *Four Weddings and a Funeral* (Hugh Grant is obsessed with his own lack of commitment). But they seem to end up together anyway.

There is a lack of an inner life with comedy characters. Because of their compulsive personalities – check out Jack Nicholson in *As Good as it Gets* – the only conflict they undergo is in trying to deal with their obsession. The audience don't want complexity.

Also, rather like sitcom, no two characters can have the same attitude towards anything that happens. This polarisation can be the ideal setting for farce. Comic characters on screen go though a learning arc. They change through the film, learning to exploit and then to deal with their personal problems and coming out better people in the end.

British comedy and film

The UK has a long and impressive history of comedy: the Ealing greats (*Passport to Pimlico*, *Whisky Galore*, *The Lavender Hill Mob*); the *St Trinian's* movies; the *Carry On* series; *Monty Python*; Mike Leigh's prestigious output. Then in the eighties, *Gregory's Girl*; *Withnail and I*; *Local Hero*; *Letter to Brezhnev*; and *Clockwise*. The nineties brought *A Fish Called Wanda*; the Richard Curtis/Working Title franchise; *The Full Monty*; and *Trainspotting*. More recently films like *Shaun of the Dead* prove that comedy is a perennial.

In addition, we have taken our TV stars and put them on the big screen – from *Steptoe and Son* and *Please Sir!* to *Ali G Indahouse* and *Kevin and Perry Go*

Large. *Bean* is the highest grossing British film (in any genre) to date. It is hard to do this, however, as sitcoms have a built-in problem: the characters do not learn. In cinema, they must. This is why most of the 1970s sitcom-to-screen transitions made terrible films – they were really only extended TV episodes.

So why do many British comedies fail? Competition is one reason; the multiplex is now the norm and out of nine or so screens, a high proportion will be American fare. This is due to the arrangements

It can, nevertheless, work the other way round. *The Odd Couple* was a superb movie, which translated beautifully to sitcom. This is because the characters already fitted into that paradigm of being trapped and not moving on. In some respects the writer (Neil Simon) had merely snipped off the third act.

between distributors, making it hard for home-grown product to gain a foothold. There is also the issue of funding. The Film Council, National Lottery, Channel 4 and BBC Films part-fund most British output, but much of it must be sourced privately.

The UK film industry is too small to have a studio system – the nearest we have is Working Title, which relies on American studio money – and we do not have the tax breaks that exist for full members of the EEC. This is why many British films are shot in Ireland.

Despite this, our films, our writers and our stars do make it on the world stage – albeit without much of the acclaim they deserve.

Yobs vs. nobs

Brits still have a problem with class: put simply, we will watch the middle classes on telly but not on the big screen. The vast majority of British films are either about yobs or nobs. Bridget Jones came from a well-off family to whom she could turn if ever in real trouble, plus everyone in Richard Curtis Land seems to be related to some earl or duke.

On the other side of the coin, Mike Leigh, Shane Meadows and Guy Ritchie seek out the lower strata of society, especially the dissolute, the under- or criminal classes.

All northern-set films are about the noble, struggling poor – *Billy Liar*, *Brassed Off*, *The Full Monty*, *Billy Elliot* and *East is East*. Am I generalising?

Yes, but audiences are very particular about what they will and will not pay to see in a British movie, which is why writing horror is often a safer bet (this genre comes with a built-in audience).

Shaun of the Dead fused genres in this way; at once a romantic comedy and a genre parody. It also succeeded in making the middling slacker characters that you might find in *Clerks* attractive to a paying crowd. This movie's success was not simply built on their TV following. *The League of Gentlemen's Apocalypse* has also used the horror parody as a starting point.

However, apart from these notable and exciting exceptions, the British public remains resolutely stick-in-the-mud when it comes to the home-grown product at the cinema.

Writing a screenplay

A screenplay is a story told with pictures: a blueprint of a film that has yet to be made. In short it is a tale about a man or a woman who *wants* something and how they either succeed or fail in obtaining it. One page of screenplay equates to one minute of screen time: comedies ought to remain short, weighing in at around the ninety minute/page mark. A rough word count is 20–25,000 words.

As with all comedy writing we begin with the concept. Once you have decided on your big idea, refer to the genres mentioned at the beginning of this Part and see where yours fits in. Each has its conventions.

Be aware of budgetary limitations. Most British films are made on a shoestring and this does not allow for a big cast or special effects. Think of a small contained story. *Clockwise* travelled from a headmaster's office to a conference. Ninety per cent of *Reservoir Dogs* (a black comedy) took place in one location.

> **With parody you'll need to keep to the original source – though not so close as to plagiarise. With romantic comedy, your star-crossed couple must be kept apart until the end. A caper will involve much careful plotting, double-crossing and revenge.**

The screenplay is written in dialogue and description. There are no inner thoughts (voiceover or flashback is believed to weaken the story). The dialogue is centred on the page, with character names above each section of speech. No single speech ought to go on for more than a few lines. Like the comedy play, the screenplay is divided into scenes – a new time or location is a new scene – and acts, which are much larger blocks of action.

There are three acts. The first is the beginning or set-up – twenty pages to tell us everything we need to know about the protagonist (lead character), his background and all the necessary information to lead us into the story. After this there is a plot point, usually a catalyst that throws him or her out of their ordinary life and into a comic adventure.

After this there is no return. It's like leaving home for university. One fine example is *Groundhog Day*.

ACT ONE
Weatherman Phil Connors (Bill Murray) goes to Punxatawney, Philadelphia to report on the arrival – or not – of an early spring, as indicated by a groundhog. Afterwards, he tries to leave, only to be thwarted by snow. He awakes the next day to find himself trapped in the same day. This set-up has prepared the audience for the next act.

ACT TWO
The middle or second act is the longest and contains the main confrontations. This is all about conflict as events conspire to keep the hero from

attaining his goal. In *Groundhog Day*, Bill Murray's character is first excited by his discovery, then depressed, then he tries a plethora of ways to win over the girl (Andie MacDowell). Towards the end of act two, the hero will reach the lowest of the low points. There is then a symbolic death, following which he is metaphorically reborn and armed with a stronger sense of purpose in order to finish his quest.

ACT THREE

Act three of *Groundhog Day* is all about winning the girl by becoming a better person. This is the resolution. Often in comedies this is short (sometimes no more than five pages) – a big twist to resolve the story and to tie up all the loose ends. Typically in romantic comedy it's where the main character realises what he has lost or wanted all along and runs to get the girl. He's always running; to the airport, the train station, usually in the rain, usually commandeering cabs, rarely cycling. When he gets there he must now convince the object of his desires that he is after all worthy. And she accepts. Ninety-nine per cent of all comedies have a happy ending. Don't forget, they are designed to make us feel better about life.

A screenplay can be further broken down into sequences and scenes. A sequence is a series of scenes tied together by a single idea. This can be something like rescuing the girl or breaking into the bank. Scenes are the individual building blocks of action, description and dialogue which are intended to move the story forwards. These can be as long as three pages or as short as a few lines.

Comic screenplays:

🖋 have a three act structure

🖋 are about characters with a blind obsession

🖋 must fit into a comic genre

🖋 if written about Britain must take note of class

🖋 are shorter than other films, coming in at around ninety pages of script

---

Other archetypal characters will people your plot. Aside from the hero there will be an advisor or mentor, the antagonist or nemesis, a threshold guardian (for example the father of the bride), shape shifters, tricksters and shadows. Much more can be read about screenplay in two excellent books, which are bibles for screenwriters: *The Writer's Journey* by Christopher Vogler and *Screenplay* by Syd Field.

Comedic screenplays are not about mere gags (with the exception of the early Zucker brothers parodies), but obsessed, funny characters who are presented with their darkest fears. It is from this situation that the comedy arises. As with sitcom (and the novel) you first create the drama, then layer on the comedy – twisting, turning and wrong-footing our and the characters' expectations.

ays write from the heart.
- Strong central character
- Sub-plot?

THINGS TO CONSIDER
• Finding an agent
• Overcoming writer's block
• ...riter should always
• ...a notebook & pen.

Part 4
Published comedy

Joke books

THE JOKE BOOK industry is surviving and thriving. Whilst many early humour collections were offshoots of *Punch* magazine, the TV spin-off has remained a constant since the 1970s, from *Monty Python's Big Red Book* and *The Goodies* to *Not the Nine O'clock News* and, more recently, *Ali G*. Although the former were written by the stars themselves, the latter were team-written. There is also a market for published scripts (for example, *Little Britain* and *The Office*) so if your show is a hit, you may be able to reap the benefits.

For the novice, there is also the huge '*Little Book of…*' industry. In most major bookstores or record outlets you will find these neat, gift size joke guides on anything from drinking to boyfriends to bling. I know, I wrote some of them. It is getting harder to find new angles for these but they do keep cropping up.

Also there are spoofs: these usually ape a current publishing (or motion picture) sensation, such as *The Lord of the Rings*, *Eats, Shoots and Leaves* or *The Da Vinci Code*. There are various so-called guides such as the *Xenophobe's Guide* series of travel books, and finally good old-fashioned joke books on all subjects from jokes for kids to *VIZ* comic's hilarious and profane output.

The comedy book market continually needs good strong ideas that will sustain readers' attention throughout a hundred pages and appeal to a broad market. Remember that these books are bought as gifts and as default presents for difficult-to-buy-for people. They invariably end up as loo reading. They are often bought for people who 'like a joke' so if you've got a loo-full at home this is testament to your wonderful sense of humour.

The comedy novel

NOVELS ARE THE most arduous form of writing, requiring careful thought, planning and research and, in my experience, at least a year in the writing. Yet if you have developed an interest for comedy writing but have found the sketch, sitcom or screenplay restricting, then maybe this is one for you.

> **The advantage of the comic novel is that you can get right inside the mind of your characters. Whatever they feel, you feel – and vice versa. They have a voice, opinions, moods and an inner life.**

As an author you can commentate on the world you create, using your main character as a kind of cipher or *alter ego* – none of this is possible in other forms of comic writing.

The comic aside, the quip and the rant are particular to the comic author, as well as witty observations on life, love and anything in between. It's a place for discussion. Characterisation, too, ought to be comic; that is, slightly enlarged or extreme. Thackeray and Dickens used it, as do Martin Amis and Carl Hiaasen. You exaggerate the physical foibles, setting up hilarious images in the mind of the reader.

The novel has a similar purity to stand-up. It is as direct in its impact on the reader as the gag is to the listener. The sitcom, the play and the screenplay are bound by description and dialogue and are interpreted by others. Your words in the novel go directly to the end user. You are the god of your creation, deciding on the complexities of your characters; on how much they tell us, how much they lie, how much you want to expose or ridicule their foibles. You choose the amount of description, the use of vernacular and the twists and turns of plot. It is a canvas on which you can paint the broadest of strokes or the tiniest of marks.

The comic novel is not a repository for all those jokes you wrote that did not work elsewhere. I will admit to having attempted to harvest my scribbling for my novels, but in the end the characters in my books threw them out, damn them.

When approaching the comic novel, it's a good idea to first of all consider what genre might suit you. There's chick or lad lit, parody, the comedy thriller, comic sci-fi, fantasy or the comedy of manners. So many current books are sporting quotes about how 'laugh-out-loud' they are that it appears that humour is a prerequisite for all novels. In fact, most are merely amusing: the genuine laugh-out-loud page-turner is as elusive as the blockbuster thriller.

Comedy novel genres

Parody takes an existing genre and sends it up. This, as mentioned previously, can be limiting.

Chick lit is Mills and Boon by another name. A single girl/mum has a number of amusing adventures as she alternately rages against and tries to snare the opposite sex. Your lead character is usually a Cinderella type with a job she despises, but which any real woman would kill for. All men are bastards except the tall wry one she 'gets'. A happy ending is mandatory.

Lad lit was a late nineties fad, led by Nick Hornby whose books detailed men's compulsive nature (hobbies, list-making, football), their irresponsibility (lack of commitment) and tendency towards infidelity (lack of commitment). A happy ending is mandatory.

The *comedy thriller* takes the thriller genre and instead of the usual square-jawed hero creates a flawed or inept protagonist, coupled with comedy henchmen, hilarious set pieces and an outrageous denouement. There will be a convoluted plot, larger than life characters and set pieces, and a lot of blood. Often there are multiple plot strands and more often than not a love story imbedded in there somewhere.

Science fiction and *fantasy* work on similar principles to the above category but often add a level of political or social spoofing. Terry Pratchett's *Discworld* series is crucial reading. He hits all his targets whilst still being almost unlawfully funny with a marvellous light touch.

The *comedy of manners* is often concerned with middle-class preoccupations such as adultery, maternity or social order. A broad church, this is usually subsumed into general fiction. Howard Jacobson is one of its best known proponents.

It is useful to note that mass market fiction is in the main bought and read by women. Men's interests tend to dwindle beyond the thriller, until you reach the niche markets like sci-fi, fantasy horror, non-fiction (biography and history, in particular) and, of course, porn.

There are, however, many precedents for great comic writing, from Jonathan Swift to Oscar Wilde, Mark Twain, Jane Austen, P. G. Wodehouse, Jerome K. Jerome, S. J. Perelman, Woody Allen and, more recently, Carl Hiaasen, Amis (father and son), Nick Hornby and Helen Fielding.

> Novels stay in circulation, can be reprinted and have a long shelf life in libraries. A novel is by far the longest and most sustained piece of writing that a comedy writer can attempt, and the satisfaction is immense in seeing your book on the shelves. One other benefit is that novels can be adapted for television (for which you will be paid again) and 80 per cent of all screenplays are sourced from novels.

The idea and the synopsis

First ask: what is it I want to write about? Is it a high concept blockbuster or an intimate family story? Either way, you will have to be as commercial about your ideas as the editor is who takes them on. Who would want to read this story?

If your answer is 'Well, everybody', you aren't focusing. In these days of demographics and marketing, you must put your energies into selling the idea first. Go to your local bookshop and see how the cover design, title, colours and typefaces can influence what you purchase. Comic novels are bright and breezy and often there is a strapline on the cover which will tell you the idea in a sentence. Write the strapline for your book. Define your genre. Say it out loud as if you were discussing the book with an editor. There is no room for prosaic description.

Assuming that you have a strong idea for a book, who are the people in it? Who is your protagonist? Is he or she sympathetic? Are we going to identify with him on his adventures? Will we care if she succeeds or fails, lives or dies? There may be an element of autobiography in your first novel, which is only natural because we do start writing from our own experience. Are you going to be interesting enough (in your *alter ego* state) to fill an entire novel? The trap is to write a plethora of funny thoughts and gags instead of constructing a character from the ground up. Use your experience wisely, be honest and true, and you can't go far wrong.

Literary fiction starts with character whereas thrillers and crime begin with the plot. Have you got your plot yet, or just the people? Is this the burning novel you have always wanted to write? If not, write that one. You are only going to go the distance if you have a close and sustained relationship to the piece.

The next stage is to write a synopsis. This is a dozen or so pages that tell the basic outline of the story. It might only be a few sentences for each chapter or it could be fifty pages of detailed character notes, dialogue and scenes. I recommend you have a synopsis to refer to just as you would not start a journey without first looking at a map. Some writers like to begin with the idea and explore it in the book, knowing that the correct resolution will eventually present itself; others like to see it plotted out first and to work creatively within that framework. Only by trying out a synopsis first will you know which one you are.

Writing a novel

Set aside certain times of the day and week for writing and *only writing*. Accept no excuse from others or from yourself for not meeting that all-important deadline. It does not matter if you write rubbish for an hour as writing is always rewriting and the process has to begin somewhere. A novel has to grow and for that you will need long, sustained hours at the screen. Maybe you write best in the morning before work. Maybe it's in the afternoon before the kids get home or even late at night. You will, because of the sheer scale of work involved, have to be prepared also to give up the TV, your social life and other personal luxuries if you are to reach the finishing line.

To write a novel, allow yourself a year from start to completion. In practise it will probably be longer, as you will want to keep rewriting until you are totally satisfied. The hard work is often done upfront, just as with other forms of comedy writing. The idea, characterisation and story/plot are what will take up all that time. Also, factor in all that thinking time.

You must be actively working on the novel on a daily basis. Don't allow gaps or anything other than real personal crises to interrupt this flow. A creative project like this will go off the boil if you don't keep stirring it. Having said that, your first novel ought not throw up such a problem. It ought to nag at you day and night until the thing is written.

During the first draft phase, DO NOT rewrite. Each time you boot up your laptop or PC, allow yourself maybe ten minutes to correct the previous paragraph, but then carry straight on. Go back at your peril! If you do, you will hate what you have written, start editing and possibly even give up.

Forget the self-justifications. Forget fancy, overcooked prose, ugly words or sentences and just *get the thing written*. The first draft of anything is never the final draft. Ever. And you will rewrite everything because that is the nature of the craft. The flipside of this is that every successive draft is quicker to complete until you have a hundred thousand perfect words – and they are all in the right order.

Once you have finished, congratulate yourself and enjoy the feeling. Leave the manuscript – which you will have been backing up every day on floppy disk – as it is. Take a break and then begin on the rewrites. The opening chapters are the hardest to write and to get right. They are the ones that you will sweat blood over.

Here are some more pointers for the comic novelist:

- Decide on who is telling the story. First person narrative is told only from inside the head of a protagonist – so he cannot know of external events until they happen to him. We can have a first person narrator telling the story directly to us or an omnipotent (God's eye) third person narrator. The advantage of the latter is that the novelist can get into the heads of any number of characters. We can switch scenes with alacrity.

- Don't overcrowd the book with characters. Five or six are usually enough.

- The first part of the writing is often clumsy. If you can cut out the first chapters, or at least significantly reduce them, then do so.

- Novels consist of one-third description,

one-third dialogue and one-third story. Keep your writing sparse and avoid overdone phrases or too much beautiful description. Make your dialogue brisk and believable.

Use strong verbs and don't overdo adverbs or adjectives.

'He said' and 'she said' are usually enough without telling us *how* he or she said it. The way that they said it ought to be implicit in the dialogue.

Try to hit a daily writing target. It might be 500 or 2,000 words but either way it's encouraging to see the words pile up. A full length novel is between 80,000 and 120,000 words.

The only time you remember to back up your work is when you have lost all your work. Don't let this happen. Make backing up a habit.

Chapters can be as short as a page or as long as twenty. However you do it, keep them to a consistent length.

Watch out for writing tics. 'As you might say', 'basically', 'actually' or 'know what I mean?' Other variations include 'perhaps', 'really', 'let's face it', 'at the end of the day' and 'we made our way'. Locate and edit them out – it will help your prose to flow.

Use colloquialisms and vernacular for verisimilitude, but don't overdo them. Give us a flavour of character.

Watch out for bon mots, aphorisms and beautifully crafted phrases. Often you will try to retain these little cherubs, but unfortunately you will eventually have to murder your darlings.

Research the facts you need either before you start or after you complete the first draft. It's up to you whether you fit the facts to the story or get it all right before it's written.

ays write from the heart.
- Strong central character
- Sub-plot?

THINGS TO CONSIDER
• Finding an agent.
• Overcoming writer's block
 riter should always
 a notebook & pen.

Part 5
The business of comedy

Aspects of the job

WRITING COMEDY IS not a nine to five job, nor is there a guaranteed regular income. It is famine and feast. It is periods of isolation contrasted with frantic activity when a project attracts attention or is nearing fruition. When you are in demand, it's easy to take on too much. If you get into this situation is it vital to explain to your employer that you have other work commitments, so that they can factor this in. Being professional, well organised and delivering what is required and on time is the way to keep working in comedy.

The lean times bring loneliness, uncertainty and the feeling that it's all somehow going on somewhere else. To counter this remember that producers, promoters, editors and publishers are busy people and that to remain 'in the loop' you must be the one keeping in contact, delivering quality material and taking criticism on board. You generate everything.

Keep abreast of the comedy market. Watch TV, read books, go to the theatre and cinema. These mediums are constantly moving forwards and it's your responsibility to move with them, or to be one step ahead.

Try not to cultivate negative attitudes. Some comedy writers spend a lot of time carping on about other people and their work. Picking holes, unless it's done as a useful learning exercise, gets you nowhere and if you express a lot of negativity in front of a producer it may go against you. Everyone likes to work with upbeat positive people and if they think you'll start bitching behind their backs it might cost you a writing job.

> **Rejection is part and parcel of the comedy writer's life. Not everyone loves your work nor cares as much as you do about the finely honed jokes, dialogue or characters.**

You may think they are missing the point, but it's rare that you will be able to discuss this with them. If you do get the chance, it's a good idea to listen. Being defensive gets you nowhere. They have formed their opinion and if you berate them they are more likely to become entrenched in it or resentful of having their professionalism questioned.

The most common reasons for a turn-down are that your piece was simply not for them (did not fit their brief/agenda) or there was something else similar in development. The only way to improve your chances of delivering that spot-on script is to persevere. And keep persevering.

To borrow from Kipling: accept triumph and defeat as the impostors that they are. Making your happiness wholly dependent on the moment you receive your BAFTA or British Comedy Award will only put the rest of your life in the shade. Those moments, and they will come if you stick at it, are only moments: 95 per cent of your time is spent getting on with it, so decorate your shed, study or workspace and enjoy your writing time, because that is the real reward – to do a job that absorbs you.

Writer's block

SOME WRITERS SUFFER days when it all silts up and nothing seems to flow. There seems to be no way of resolving that joke, sketch or plot. You are out of ideas. You have a deadline and you will never complete the work. You start to panic and now, instead of thinking creatively, you are obsessing over the problem.

Fallow periods are a natural part of the creative process. If a horse is not fed, watered and rested, you'll end up flogging a dead one. Panic and worry are turnaround phases in which nothing creative can flourish, so they must be dispensed with. You won't lose the next gig. You won't lose the ability to write funny. Instead, allow your batteries time to recharge by getting away from your work space. Walk. Play some sport. Engage in anything other than the task at hand. Sleep on it. Don't expect the ideas to flow. Ignore comedy altogether. A little time and distance will work wonders.

It's worth reiterating a point I made when looking at sketch writing: life rarely has punchlines. Most comic stories are exaggerations or constructs, a contrivance. This means that you will be spending much of your time trying to bolt on a punchline or trying to resolve your story so that it comes out in the funniest way. This is hard work. I usually find that the best solution is to look within the writing you have already done. Listen to your characters and let them tell you the answers. This is called *writing from the page*.

There is another kind of block that affects writers and it is more thematic. Let's say you are obsessed with an old flame. You write a sitcom about a guy obsessed with his old flame. It does not sell. You write a play about three characters who meet up in a recovery clinic for people trying to get over relationships. Turns out they are all

> You must be prepared to let things go in comedy. Trust your creations. They have the answers. If they steadfastly refuse to give up the answers you may, unfortunately, have to rethink them or, in the worst case scenario, drop the idea.

trying to get over the same woman – and one of them is a woman. You get it put on, but it doesn't really get anywhere. A year later, you start on a novel about a woman who has a one night stand but falls in love with the man. It's bittersweet because it turns out that he is obsessed with an old flame. It does not find a home with a publisher.

This is therapeutic writing, and there's nothing wrong in that – in fact any of the above projects might have sold, but the idea and writer have simply not found their time. If this happens, let it go. Get on with other things. Maybe even hunt down that old flame and confront your feelings? You never know, you might end up writing a screenplay about someone who had to lay all the ghosts of their previous exes to rest before learning to love again.

Never lose faith in your ability to write and to write funny. If you can do it once you will do it again. A gift for comedy is something we have for life.

Topical gags

WRITE TWENTY ONE-LINERS. BBC radio has a show called *Parsons and Naylor's Pull Out Section*, which is always looking for topicals. Details are on the BBC website listed at the back of this book.

Watch TV chat shows. You will notice that the ones presented by comedians invariably open with a monologue about the news. These are written gags. Watch the credits and jot down the producer's name, the script editor and the production company. Phone and ask if you can send in material. Don't e-mail; all unsolicited e-mails may be suspected of carrying viruses.

You can approach comedians or advertise your services as a topical gag writer in *The Stage* – the weekly newspaper for unemployed actors. *Contacts*, *Spotlight* and the *Writers' & Artists' Yearbook* are the best sources for finding out who represents who – again, details are in the back of this book.

Writing on spec

ALWAYS BE PREPARED to work 'on spec' (speculatively); that is, to provide samples of work for free. Producers often have a vague idea of what they are after and use writers to flesh it out. If you are the one who is willing to help in these early stages of the creative process, then you may become invaluable.

Keep samples of your writing to act as calling cards. This might be a sketch, a page of strong jokes or a whole script. Make sure that the copy you send out is 'clean' – in other words, unread and unmarked with other comedians' or actors' names.

Spec writing is a constant in all aspects of the comedy world and you will be expected to meet producers halfway on this. However, if you find yourself working for months with no sign of remuneration, then you ought to reassess your position. You may be told you are being given the opportunity of learning 'on the job', a sort of comedy work experience. This is fine so long as there is a clearly defined goal and a written promise that you will be credited should a commission arise. If in doubt, try consulting the Writers' Guild.

Always put your name, address and contact details on everything you send out.

Always enclose a polite – and never funny – covering letter.

Always log what you send and to whom you have sent it, and follow up with a polite enquiry after not less than a month. If a producer asks for more examples of your work or for a rewrite, then deliver this promptly.

Keep in contact with other writers and with editors, readers and producers. You never know what this may produce. None of those people are directly responsible for the financial side of the business, although the producer does control the budget and will know how much can be apportioned to the writer(s). Discussion of actual fees, contracts and residual payments is done via the finance and legal departments and it is they who will contact you or your agent/representative once a project is underway.

Stand-up

IN THE STAND-UP comedy market supply far outstrips demand. This means it is highly competitive and to succeed you must offer something fresh and exciting to whet the palates of jaded bookers.

In the early years it is not paid well, but I strongly recommend that you do not ever 'pay to play'. This means paying for your stage time and it is the equivalent of vanity publishing. Promoters do need to cover their costs and it's legitimate to pay a token entry fee for a new act competition (one that offers prestige or a cash prize) but that's the only time you should part with your money to go on stage. The club owner ought to bear the costs of running his or her own business.

The 'circuit' is called that because it is cyclical. You go round and round, gaining stage experience up to the point where you can headline and/or attract management. It is easy to be dazzled by the big agencies and I recommend that you treat any offer of representation with caution. Losses higher up on the ladder are often borne by those on lower rungs and you may find yourself paying huge 'publicity' costs and for your agent's travel and accommodation expenses. If you want more advice on the comedy circuit from the horse's mouth please contact me via the Summersdale website.

Sketches

BBC RADIO 2 and 4 are the prime stations for original comedy sketch material, most of which is broadcast at 6.30 p.m. or 11 p.m. slots, along with weekend repeats. This varies, so do check listings magazines. Tune in and get a flavour of the shows and note the names of the producers. Details of how to submit your material and the preferred formats are on the BBC writersroom website. Stick to these religiously, especially the notes on formatting your work (there are several free downloads of script formats, using a programme called Script Smart). Producers are overworked and anything which looks like you have not bothered will give them an excuse to ignore your submission.

Let's assume that you have chosen the shows you would like to write for. You understand the format and have isolated the parts you're going to have a go at. Keep your sketch tight, don't overcrowd it with sound effects and keep to one scene (one time and location). Write *for* the actual stars. You will by now be familiar with their mannerisms so try to get a flavour of how they talk. If the star feels at home with the piece it will increase its chances. Be bespoke.

Don't flood them with submissions – a steady stream is best. Let them know that you are there, but don't hammer on the door. People warm slowly to newcomers and trust has to be earned. A hundred sketches will not impress whereas six or seven belters will.

Alternatively you can cold call or write to them directly. Study the credits on your favourite programmes to get

> For TV sketch writing, start by reading *Broadcast* magazine (the weekly industry newspaper) or study it online. *The Stage* gives information on shows going into production and there is an online newsletter called *PCR (Production and Casting Report)* for actors and casting directors. These are not aimed specifically at writers, but the details will help you to get in touch with production companies.

names of producers and production companies. All the indies (independent production companies) are listed in the *Writers' & Artists' Yearbook*. Call and explain that you are a new writer looking for opportunities. They may be able to put you on to someone who can help. Even a straight no is useful as it saves time sending material to companies who do not require it. Contacting broadcasters is a labyrinthine process. However, the Channel 4 and BBC writersoom websites ought to be your first port of call.

As with radio, submit a good range of your work – ten pages is enough – and be constant with volume and quality. If you are lucky enough to be given a brief (a breakdown of the targets and characters that they want to create) then write to it. A letter and contract offer will follow if your work is used.

Make sure you have your NAME and CONTACT DETAILS on every page. I have capitalised this because it is so vital. Pages get lost and separated and half a sketch that cannot be married to its punchline may be binned.

The going BBC rate for sketches is currently about the price of a night down the pub. Not a Friday night.

> **Remember:**
>
> 🖊 Read industry newspapers and online info.
>
> 🖊 Approach open submission shows.
>
> 🖊 Ask for and write to the brief. Adopt the proper formats.
>
> 🖊 Produce quality and volume.
>
> 🖊 Put your contact details on every page.
>
> 🖊 Expect to spend at least a year as a non-commissioned writer.
>
> 🖊 Contacts will help you find other work.

There is little money in radio but diligence will get your work accepted on a regular basis. If you start to get things on every other week, it won't be long before the producer invites you in for a chat. The outcome of this may be a commission for a regular number of 'minutes' a week, meaning that you will write a number of sketches on a given topic, and be guaranteed a fee.

Becoming a commissioned writer has many advantages. You know what is and isn't being covered, and you are given a specific task rather than writing blind. Weekly meetings will give you a chance to meet other writers and producers. This is a good professional step because radio producers are busy with multiple projects and when they're looking for writers they tend not to stray far from the nest. Also, they often move on to telly. If you are looking to expand your comedy writing into creating your own shows, these are the people who can help shape and put them in front of a commissioning head. Other writers will also know of other opportunities, can recommend you, collaborate and, of course, gossip.

Finding out about upcoming TV sketch shows is hard, as writing posts are not advertised. The usual way they come about is that a producer or production company has been putting the show together with the head writers and stars and it has been green-lit (commissioned). Six episodes are ordered and the head writers are furiously scribbling away. The number of writers needed depends on the nature of the show. *Spitting Image* and *Naked Video* were fairly open-door (anyone could have a go) but *Monkey Dust* and *Alistair McGowan's Big Impression* are a closed shop. This is because the creators wanted to keep a tight rein on their product. However, as series progress, they are more likely to open up the books to new writers.

Increasingly, groups of sketch writers and performers are putting on their own sketch shows or making their own 'taster tapes' of programmes. This is done to attract an independent production company and/or broadcaster and can either be live or recorded. To do it live, you may put on a show at a fringe theatre or take a show to the Edinburgh Festival – more on that follows.

> If you want to film your show, use minimal locations and cast and get a good DV (digital video) camera. Shoot a 'taster' of fifteen minutes of sketches and do make sure you have separate sound as in-built microphones tend to pick up all sorts of extraneous noise.

If you are going to spend money, spend it on a sound technician and an editor, not on flashy graphics. Once you are satisfied with the results, convert your DV tape to video cassette, label it with your contact details and send it to a selection of the independent production companies whom you will have selected from the *Writers' & Artists' Yearbook* (check they will accept tapes). Include a short covering letter detailing the format of the show and both your CV and those of the cast.

If you are thinking of radio, you will need to do a recording on cassette or on CD. Once you are happy with your script, get the best actors you can and rehearse like mad before booking any studio spaces. A good sound engineer is worth his considerable weight in gold and studio time is not cheap. If you want to do it at home on the PC, the programme you will need is Adobe Audition (a good multi-track programme formerly known as Cool Edit Pro). Sound quality is dependent on how much you spend on microphones and a mixing desk. With the right equipment, it is possible for the amateur to achieve sound quality of broadcast standards, which will impress the listener. The submission process is the same as for sending film, although there are fewer independents who supply to radio. You may also send it to producers at BBC Radio Light Entertainment, since BBC Radio is currently the main comedy market.

There is a growing stream of comedy on the Internet, but as yet no evidence of anyone being paid. Sketches are what they are looking for, so it might be a good test bed for you. Ultimately, if you do place a show on the Net, speak to the Writers' Guild about your rights and permissions.

Another way of advertising yourself as a comedian or sketch or comic playwright is to take a show to the Edinburgh Fringe Festival.

Edinburgh

YOU WILL NOT make money in Edinburgh. If you are lucky you may only lose a couple of thousand, but you may incur much higher costs. The month-long run during August is seen as the world's cultural trade fair, but venue hire is costly, and you will need to sell at between 60 and 80 per cent capacity for your show to break even. Most shows get an average of 12 paying punters. On top of that there is PR and publicity and then accommodation and living costs, which are sky high.

You will hopefully get reviewed – not by professional critics, but by people who have been drafted in to cover the Festival or have been moved from other duties (the usual joke is that they are the gardening correspondent). These reviews mean little, but

> Edinburgh does, however, retain its cachet, and if you build up a reputation by going for two or three years, then people will get to know your work. You will also be in the epicentre of a thriving, creative, cultural melting pot in which you'll meet like-minded others and make contacts.

the good lines in them can be used on the posters for your next show. You will also get drunk. Very drunk.

How do you put on a show if you cannot afford to lose thousands? One option is to tailor your work so as to attract sponsorship. Beer and comedy go together well and breweries often tie in with comics. Can you theme a show so as to appeal to sponsors? Remember that businesses like comedy promotions as they believe it humanises them. The cuddly, caring face of capitalism, if you will.

A second option allows you to avoid the cartel of venues, promoters and agents who have sewn up the Festival. Luckily, this monopoly is changing – most significantly with the rise of the Free Fringe. Instead of paying out vast sums to managers and venue owners, the space comes gratis so long as the show is offered free – donations are collected at the end. This is a welcome return to the spirit of the Fringe. You don't poster the town or have agents herd the press and TV people into the biggest venues; instead, you flyer like mad, put on a great little play, sketch or stand-up show and learn without losing your shirt.

More information on the Free Fringe and on how to apply to the Edinburgh Fringe is available at the back of the book.

Plays

YOU CAN PUT on a play at Edinburgh, at London fringe venues, local arts centres/studio spaces or with amateur dramatics companies. Costs vary, but so long as you keep the cast, props and costumes minimal your main expenses will be venue hire and promotion. These can be kept in the low hundreds. You can source theatre producers from the *Writers' & Artists' Yearbook* and invite them and literary agents to see your work. You will not hit the West End immediately. If your play is taken on it's likely to be tried out in the provinces or in a limited London run at a small prestigious venue like the Gate, Bush or Soho theatres.

There are also bursaries and competitions, and many theatres run their own incentive schemes for new writers. Read the applications and regulations carefully and fulfil them to the letter. If your play does succeed then you will be looking at receiving somewhere around five per cent of the total net box office receipts for each and every performance.

Sitcom/comedy drama

SEND OUT THE second episode of any sitcom, but the first (pilot) of a comedy drama. Always send outlines for the other episodes in the series. Keep your character breakdowns minimal and include in your covering letter a one paragraph 'pitch' for the show (like a blurb on the back cover of a book).

If a reader sees potential in your show, he will then give it to a producer who will make a decision on whether

Send the script and the covering letter out to the independent production companies, who all have script reading departments and external readers. Alternatively, you might enter the BBC 3, Channel 4 or Channel 5 competitions for sitcom writers. These are often trailed on TV and are mentioned on the relevant websites.

or not to invite you in. This may mean they are going to option your script. If your sitcom or comedy drama idea is optioned by a production company or broadcaster, this means that they are buying the right to develop it. For this you will be paid a tenth of the total price of the script. The option means that they now have a year to eighteen months to try and sell it to a network. During this time you will then be expected to work with them on the rewrites, for which you ought to be paid.

If they sell it to a network you'll receive the balance and more to write another script or two. Once the show is green-lit you'll get paid for all six – or however many are specified in the series.

Once you are on the bandwagon, your writing fees will rise often by as much as 25 per cent for each successive project. Huge sums are paid to 'name writers' (writers whose names are more important than the actors or the project itself) and often they are tied into remunerative development deals.

Screenplays

IN FILM, IT is said that one in ten treatments (ten to twelve pages detailing the whole story) sells. One in ten of those sold is developed. One in ten of those developed is shot. Seven out of ten films shot are turkeys, two make their money back and one is a blockbuster.

Screenplays, like sitcoms, are also optioned, sometimes from a treatment but, more usually for the first timer, from the whole script. (Never offer anyone a free option.) This deal will include staggered payments for the delivery of the first draft script, the second and polishes. Again, these start low and rise to the high five figures. The balance of your fee for the script is payable on the first day of principal photography.

Worst case scenario is you get some money to develop the script, do several months' (paid) work on it, but they put it into turnaround. This means the script stays in a holding pattern, waiting to be picked up again as they search for funding. During this time your option may expire (the time runs out). In this case they will either renew or they will let it drop.

If the latter happens, you are free to sell the piece all over again. However, be aware that the work you did with them – the drafts, the changes in plot or characters – remains their property. It's the original that you can sell on. This is not the same for a novel or play, where your final draft is set in stone.

Submitting the comedy book

To SUBMIT A comedy book idea you need a good one. Research your market carefully first so that you do not clash with an existing product. Think it through. Is this going to appeal to a broad market? Is it too broad? Too narrow? Too unfocused? Can you see it on the bookshelves?

You will need to write some 'blurb' – a witty paragraph describing the book, its contents and format, and then either a sample chapter or – if it's all jokes – ten to fifteen gags that you intend to use. This ought to be enough for an editor to make a decision. Approaching editors is best covered in the book *How to be a Writer*, also in this series.

Your jokes must be fresh and original. There is no excuse for downloading them from the Internet, and any publisher who becomes aware of this will be highly miffed. When you sign any publishing contract it is on the proviso that it is your own work, and you are responsible for clearing any rights to quotes or to other material that is not wholly your own. Plagiarism and intellectual property rights are touchy subjects and this area is no exception. There are indeed joke books out there that are no more than hastily cobbled together 'highlights' but these exist because the material is either so old or so familiar that it is considered to be in the public domain. It is not safe to assume that because something is on the Net it is up for grabs. It is best to always generate your own. For advice on where to submit, see the section on selling your work.

Remember:

🖋 The concept is most important. It must capture popular tastes.

🖋 Write a page of 'blurb' describing your book and what it will contain.

🖋 Write at least fifteen joke samples, or a sample chapter.

🖋 Don't plagiarise.

🖋 Parody is competitive.

Submitting the comedy novel

THE PROCESS FOR submitting a comedy novel is the same as it is for submitting any kind of novel. Pay attention to the following guidelines.

When you have completed the third or fourth draft of your book, you will start to feel like you are 'there'. Some perfectionists continue way after this point, because they are terrified of releasing anything into the wide world that is not a shining diamond. Although this is admirable, the truth is that nothing is ever perfect and every manuscript is subject to readers', editors', copy-editors' and other critical eyes before it reaches the public. Accepting this is important, just as you must not send out something half-baked. There will come a time when you have rewritten your novel to the point where all you're doing is tinkering. That is the time to stop. It's ready.

An agent's or a publisher's slush pile – it's up to you. Having completed and polished the novel, you must submit according to the agent's or publisher's guidelines. Send the whole manuscript with a covering letter, describing the project in a couple of simple sentences and anything about you as the author that you feel is relevant. It will take a long time for you to hear back from them, maybe months. Some specify that they do not want phone calls. Don't pester them with e-mails. They will read it and they will get back to you. Eventually.

If, sadly, your novel does not strike a chord, examine the rejection letter for clues. If it's terse or seems standard then perhaps your writing isn't up to scratch yet, but if they offer reasons take heed. Many great novels were turned down at first. Perhaps the market isn't ready for this kind of book. Perhaps there is no market. Perhaps they recently bought something similar. You must always use your negatives to lead to the positive.

> **Congratulations! A call or a letter arrives suggesting a meeting to discuss your book. This means that they want to check out that you are who you say you are and that they are probably going to offer to publish you. You may even get lunch.**

Once you have secured a publishing deal you will be offered an advance, which is money set against future sales. If the sales of the book do not equal the advance you will not have to give it back. Never pay to publish a book. As you are a new author, they might want to offer you a two book deal – meaning that you will get some money up front for your second novel as well – so you'd better have something to talk about, even if it is only in the planning stages.

More on getting a novel published may be found in another book in this series, *How to get Published*.

Agents

YOU HAVE NO need of an agent if you are writing for stand-up or broken comedy, unless the latter is of such volume that you need a negotiator. At this point you want to find someone who will sell your work and gain exposure for it. Agents have clout, will negotiate and can offer career advice. You need to be represented by someone who is passionate about your work and this narrows down the field. First you'll need an agent who is a fan of and who moves in the comedy industry. There are several ways of going about finding an agent:

- Cold calling.

- Sending in your work on spec. This leads to the slush pile but it is the most common way – sending your work to everyone. Some agencies may ask if the work is being read by anyone else. Of course it is. Be truthful. You are trying to run a business and you must maximise your options in seeking representation.

- Dialogue with a producer. This is a great route, because it's both an 'in' and a recommendation.

- To be recommended by another client of the agency.

- To be recommended by another agent in the company.

It is still hard to get an agent even if you are selling your work. This is because competition is fierce and slush piles are enormous. They are always searching for reasons to say no, so don't make that job easy for them. Don't overload them with work. One or two samples are fine. Send out quality and volume and be patient and persevere; the right agent will come to you at the right time. To show you why it's not personal, here are a few of the reasons why they aren't 'hiring right now':

- The agent is not taking on any new clients.

- His taste does not coincide with your style of writing.

- He does not specialise in sitcom/plays/novels/comedy…

- It's the wrong time of year.

- He is about to leave the agency.

Here is what agents are looking for:

- Someone with talent and originality.

- Someone approachable, friendly and easy to deal with.

- Someone who has longevity, maturing over many years.

- Someone whose writing will make them a large amount of money, thereby offsetting the ones whose writing doesn't.

In return, here is what you can expect from an agent:

- To return your calls within a reasonable amount of time.

- To pay all outstanding fees promptly and fully.

- To read what you send him and offer a fair opinion.

- To send out your work or have a good reason for not doing so.

✐ To get your work read.

✐ To be well versed in and up to date in contractual minutiae and contract law as regards your area of writing.

✐ To prepare and complete all your negotiations, including options and script sales, and to keep his finger on residuals and world market arrangements.

✐ To have a good reputation so that the above happens in good time.

✐ To step in for you when there are disputes over payments or other business issues pertaining to your writing career.

✐ To have a good current knowledge of developments in your area and for current project needs.

✐ To discuss with you your future prospects as a writer.

He or she is not your editor, friend, parent, confidant or confessor. Once you have an agent you have a good calling card, but they will not do the job for you. If a piece of work is not going to sell then there is nothing they can do for it. Some people have friendly relationships with their agents and stay with them for many years, others chop and change, and others never use an agent at all. You can register with the Writers' Guild and use their facilities, plus Equity members have access to free or cheap legal advice.

Resources

Courses

City University
Northampton Square
London EC1V 0HB
020 7040 5060
020 7040 5070 (fax)
www.city.ac.uk/conted/cfa/write/media
Writing comedy and situation comedy courses

Associations

WGGB (The Writers' Guild of Great Britain)
The Writers' Guild of Great Britain
15 Britannia Street
London WC1X 9JN
http://writersguild.org.uk
Offers a pension scheme, free legal advice, free access to ALCS (Authors' Licensing and Collecting Service) and quarterly magazine *The Writer*.
Membership £90 annually.

The Agents' Association (GB)
54 Keyes House
Dolphin Square
London SW1V 3NA
020 7834 0515
020 7821 0261 (fax)
www.agents-uk.com/contact.html
E-mail: association@agents-uk.com

Studio tickets

BBC Studio Audiences
PO Box 3000
BBC TV Centre
London W12 7RJ
020 8576 1227
www.bbc.co.uk/comedy/tickets/index.shtml

Books

Screenplay: The Foundations of Screenwriting
Syd Field
(Bantam Doubleday Dell Publishing Group, 1987,
ISBN 0440576474)

The Writer's Journey: Mythic Structure for Storytellers and Screenwriters
Christopher Vogler
(Pan, 1999, ISBN 0330375911)

Writers' & Artists' Yearbook
(A & C Black Ltd, ISBN 0713666595)
www.acblack.com

Recommended scripts

Blackadder – The Whole Damn Dynasty, Richard Curtis, Ben Elton, Rowan Atkinson and John Lloyd (Penguin, 1999)

The Best of Frasier, 15 scripts from the first series by numerous writers (Channel 4 Books, 1999)

Radio Times Guide to TV Comedy, Mark Lewisohn (BBC Worldwide, 1998)

Websites

www.marcblake.greatnow.com

Robin Kelly's writing for performance website
has many courses:
www.writing.org.uk

British Society of Comedy Writers
www.bscw.co.uk

Final Draft
Software for script writing in all forms. Available in
UK from the Screenwriters Store or try:
www.finaldraft.com

BBC writersroom
New Writing Coordinator
3rd floor, 1 Mortimer Street
London W1T 3JD
020 7765 2703 020 7765 0243 (script tracking)
new.writing@bbc.co.uk
www.bbc.co.uk/writersroom/
Open door policy for BBC radio shows. Also Script
Smart downloads.

Newsrevue
www.newsrevue.com

Edinburgh Festival
www.edfringegroups.com
www.freefringe.com

Online publications

Broadcast
www.broadcastnow.co.uk

The Stage
www.thestage.co.uk

PCR
www.pcrnewsletter.com.

For further information and to contact me:

www.summersdale.com

How to get Published
Secrets from the Inside
Stewart Ferris

The concept that a good book will always find a publisher is outdated and over-simplistic. The sad truth is that most writers remain unpublished because they pay attention *only* to the quality of their writing. Publishers are business people. Their job is to make money from selling books. They know that high quality writing alone isn't always enough to make a profitable book, so when choosing which manuscripts to sign up for publication they think about many more elements than just the words on the page.

After 15 years in the book industry, **Stewart Ferris** has identified all of the crucial factors that publishers consider besides good writing. *How to Get Published* reveals for the first time these inside secrets and provides tactics that any writer can use to create the perfect conditions for their own 'lucky break' to happen.

Stewart Ferris has published 500 books, rejected 10,000 submissions, and is the author of more than 20 books.

How to be a Writer
Secrets from the Inside
Stewart Ferris

Many people who call themselves writers don't produce enough words in a year to fill a postcard. Other writers churn out thousands of words but never sell their work. This book tackles both problems: it gets you writing, easily and painlessly guiding you through the dreaded 'writer's block'; and it divulges industry secrets that will help you to raise the quality of your work to a professional level.

In fact, there is only one major difference between writers who get paid for their work and writers who only collect rejections. This difference is something that anyone can fix and is revealed in this book along with essential rules and conventions that will launch your writing career.

During 14 years' experience in the publishing industry **Stewart Ferris** has published 500 books, rejected 10,000 manuscripts and has written more than 20 books that have been translated into 6 languages. He has also written for stage, film, television and radio.